Bible STORY BASICS Scope & Sequence | Fall

MW00534378

Fall 2019	Winter 2019–20	Spring 2020	Summer 2020
UNIT 1: Beginnings **Genesis 1:31**	**UNIT 1: Hope** **Isaiah 2:5**	**UNIT 1: Journey** **Psalm 121:8**	**UNIT 1: Paul** **Philippians 4:13**
1. Creation Genesis 1:1-25	1. Swords into Plows Isaiah 2:1-5	1. Man in the Synagogue Matthew 12:9-14	1. Paul's Conversion Acts 9:1-20
2. God's Image Genesis 1:26–2:4a	2. Mary's Story Luke 1:26-38, 46-47	2. Jesus and the Children Matthew 19:13-15	2. Love in Action Romans 12:9-18
3. Adam and Eve Genesis 2:4b–3:24	3. Joseph's Story Matthew 1:18-24	3. Last Supper Matthew 26:17-30	3. Paul Escapes Acts 9:20-25
4. Noah Genesis 6:1–9:17	4. Jesus' Story Luke 2:1-7	4. In the Garden Matthew 26:31-56	4. Be Glad and Endure Philippians 4:4-14
5. Tower of Babel Genesis 11:1-9	5. Shepherds' Story Luke 2:8-20	5. Peter Matthew 26:57-58, 69-75	
UNIT 2: Ancestors **Genesis 15:5**	**UNIT 2: Calling** **Matthew 4:19**	**UNIT 2: Alleluia** **Matthew 28:7**	**UNIT 2: Leaders** **2 Timothy 1:7**
6. Abraham and Sarah Genesis 12:1-9; 15:1-6	6. Follow the Star Matthew 2:1-12	6. Hosanna! Matthew 21:1-11; 27:32-66	5. Be a Leader Acts 16:1-5; 1 Tim. 4:7b-16
7. Abraham and Lot Genesis 13:1-12	7. Jesus Is Baptized Matthew 3:13-17	7. Easter Matthew 28:1-10	6. Be Encouraged 2 Timothy 1:3-7
8. The Birth of Isaac Genesis 18:1-15; 21:1-7	8. Jesus Calls the Fishermen Matthew 4:18-22	8. Breakfast on the Beach John 21:1-19	7. Lydia Acts 16:11-15
9. Isaac and Rebekah Genesis 24:1-67	9. Beatitudes Matthew 5:1-12	9. The Great Commission Matthew 28:16-20	8. Paul and Silas Acts 16:16-40
UNIT 3: Blessings **Genesis 28:14**	**UNIT 3: Wisdom** **Matthew 7:24**	**UNIT 3: Believers** **Acts 2:4**	**UNIT 3: Prophets** **1 Kings 18:39**
10. Jacob and Esau Genesis 25:19-28	10. The Lord's Prayer Matthew 6:5-15	10. Believers Share Acts 4:32-37	9. Elijah and the Ravens 1 Kings 16:29-30; 17:1-7
11. The Birthright Genesis 25:29-34	11. The Birds in the Sky Matthew 6:25-34	11. Choosing the Seven Acts 6:1-7	10. Elijah and the Prophets 1 Kings 18:20-39
12. The Blessing Genesis 27:1-46	12. The Golden Rule Matthew 7:12	12. Philip and the Ethiopian Acts 8:26-40	11. Elijah and Elisha 1 Kings 19:1-21
13. Jacob's Dream Genesis 28:10-22	13. The Two Houses Matthew 7:24-27	13. First Called "Christians" Acts 11:19-30	12. Elisha and the Widow 2 Kings 4:1-7
		14. Pentecost Acts 2:1-41	13. Elisha and Naaman 2 Kings 5:1-19a

Contents

Bible STORY BASICS

- unleashes the power of God's Word to work in the minds and hearts of children;

- establishes the Bible as foundational in children's lives and faith;

- equips both leaders and children to read, appreciate, and understand Scripture and its historical context and enduring message; and

- provides children a depth of spiritual resources to draw upon in difficult times.

Check out
www.biblestorybasics.com
to stay up to date on all the
Bible Story Basics news.

Written by Daphna Flegal.
Cover design by Ed Maksimowicz. Illustrations by Ralph Voltz.

Art—pp. 12, 18, 24, 85, 93, 94: Shutterstock®; p. 30: Mernie Gallagher-Cole/Portfolio Solutions; p. 36: Susan Harrison; p. 42: Kimberly Soderberg/Deborah Wolfe Ltd.; p. 48: Mandy France/Gwen Walters Artist Rep.; p. 54: Carol Schwartz/Portfolio Solutions; p. 60, 66: Abingdon curriculum; p. 72: Brian Parker; p. 78, 84: Linda Pierce/Gwen Walters Artist Rep.; pp. 88, 89, 90: Diana Magnuson; p. 91, 92, 95: Robert S. Jones.

Welcome to

We're glad you're here! This year you and your kids will journey together to discover tools for reading and learning the Bible. Your children will hear foundational Bible stories, memorize key verses, and internalize God's Word while having fun with music, games, puzzles, prayer, and more!

Bible Story Basics is a comprehensive three-year Bible study built to help children understand the overarching story of God's Word while nurturing and growing their faith—without a lot of complicated extras.

With a simple look and feel, these lessons are straightforward and easy to teach. The broad age-level structure (ages 3-7 and 8-12) makes it simple to group your children, while also providing leaders the confidence to teach age-appropriate lessons.

We invite you and your children to experience the depths of God's love expressed in the stories of the Bible. It's basic!

What Children Ages 3-7 Need

For developing faith foundations, children need	For knowing the Bible and our faith traditions, children need	For relating to God and the church, children need	For relating faith to daily living, children need
• to be with adults whose Christian attitudes and behaviors the children can imitate; • to have their feelings and actions accepted and to be forgiven when they do not meet adult expectations; • to develop and express their own identity as individuals and in relation to others; • to be guided in playing cooperatively with other children; and • to practice decision-making through optional activities.	• to handle the Bible and see others read from it; • to sing and say Bible verses, especially from Psalms and the Gospels; • to recognize the Lord's Prayer, the Golden Rule, and other affirmations of our faith; • to hear stories of Bible people who lived as God wanted them to live; • to participate in Communion with parents or other caregivers; and • to hear short stories about the church today and in the past.	• to learn simple prayers; • to be encouraged to give their own offerings to God and to the church; • to develop a sense of belonging at church and of being a child of God; • to have accepting adults who are willing to hear their many questions about God, life, death, and crises; and • to experience awe and wonder through nature, life cycles, and corporate worship, even though they may not be able to talk about the meanings of their experiences.	• to hear stories about service to others and to observe leaders, parents, and older children in service to others; • to participate in service by making things for others and by sharing money and food; • to hear leaders, parents, or guardians pray about people and situations beyond themselves; • to use Sunday school take-home items as reminders of what they learned in Sunday school; and • to practice caring for and appreciating God's world.

Using This Leader Guide

Underlying each aspect of the Bible Story Basics curriculum is the belief that all children should have the opportunity to experience the depths of God's love for them expressed in the timeless stories of the Bible. Each story-focused session allows the narrative to drive children's faith formation and provides a rich context for the development of biblical literacy skills.

Bible Background and Devotion

The first page of each Leader Guide session offers Bible background and a devotion to help the facilitator prepare for the lesson, better understand the biblical context, and spend a few moments in meditation and prayer.

Lesson Flow

B - The flow of the lesson starts with **Bible Beginnings**. This is the time to welcome the children and introduce the Bible story. Each week, the pre-readers will have a coloring picture of the Bible story and a Bible puzzle. There is also a suggestion for Bible play. Play is an important way young children learn. This activity will focus their play on the Bible story.

I - The lesson then moves **Into the Bible**. This will include two opportunities for the children to hear the Bible story, one from the *Bible Basics Storybook* and one from the week's Bible Story Leaflet. The leaflet story will be interactive. This section will also include the Bible tool, helping the children learn the Bible verse and the mechanics of the Bible.

B - Following the Bible story, the children will experience activities that help them make **Bible Connections**. These activities draw from various learning styles to present age-appropriate ideas and to help deepen the children's understanding of the Bible story.

L - Next, the lesson moves to activities that will help the children **Live the Bible** and make the Bible relevant to their own lives.

E - Finally, the lesson will close with opportunities to **Express Praise**. This section includes a song and prayer, plus suggestions for how you can bless and affirm each child.

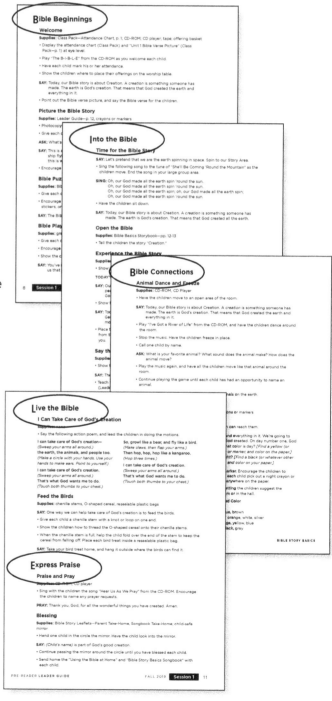

Resources

Leader Guide

This guide features 13 low-prep and step-by-step session guides that offer creative ways for children to experience foundational Bible stories through a variety of learning styles.

Bible Story Leaflets

These leaflets feature colorful and realistic art from Ralph Voltz and offer creative ways to involve children in the Bible story and to facilitate a connection between church and home with weekly questions and prayers to share as a family.

Class Pack

The annual Class Pack includes 12 Bible verse pictures to assist in Scripture memorization, a CD-ROM containing music and additional teaching materials, and an attendance chart. The additional teaching materials on the CD-ROM are also available to download at *biblestorybasics.com/resources*.

Student Take-Home CD

This CD includes seven memorable songs for the children to learn and enjoy throughout the year. The CD is sold in packs of five at a price that makes it possible to send one home with each child.

Bible Basics Storybook

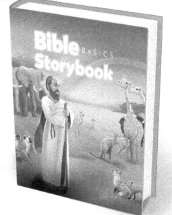

The 149 Old and New Testament stories in this storybook will invite your child into the Word through beautiful illustrations, retellings that are appropriate for young children, and prayers that connect to our faith.

Bible Story Basics resources are available in Braille on request.

Contact:
Braille Ministry
c/o Donna Veigel
10810 N. 91st Avenue #96
Peoria, AZ 85345
(623)-979-7552

Supplies

No matter what activities you choose to use, there are some basic supplies you likely will need at some point. Collect these supplies and keep them accessible every Sunday.

The Basics

- baby dolls
- CD player
- CEB Bibles
- chenille stems
- child-safe mirror
- clear tape
- construction paper
- cotton balls
- crayons
- glue
- markers
- masking tape
- newsprint
- offering basket
- paper bowls
- paper cups
- paper plates
- pencils
- plain paper
- plastic table covering
- play dough
- posterboard
- scissors
- spoons
- stapler
- star stickers
- tray
- washable paint

Beyond the Basics

Once you have chosen the activities in each session that you intend to do, check the specific supplies for each activity.

If some of the necessary supplies are slightly out of the ordinary, make a wish list of the supplies you will need. Publish the list in the church newsletter or bulletin. Members of your church will be happy to know how they can support the children in the church.

If you have a place to store supplies, encourage the congregation to bring the supplies you will need for the rest of the quarter. If you do not have a place to store things, make a new list each week of the things you will need in the next two or three weeks.

Creation

Bible Verse: God saw everything he had made: it was supremely good. (Genesis 1:31)

Bible Story: Genesis 1:1-25

Bible Background

What better way to begin a new Sunday school year than at the beginning? Our Bible story for today comes from the first chapter of the first book of the Bible—Genesis. Genesis contains two accounts of Creation, one in the first chapter and one in the second chapter. There are many similarities between the two accounts. It has been suggested that the second account may have been an attempt to provide more detail to certain aspects of the story. We will look at the first account over the next two weeks and then look at the second account on week three.

There is a definite rhythm to the Creation story in Genesis 1. God speaks. Creation happens. God evaluates.

First, God spoke: "Let there be light" and "Let there be a dome in the middle of the waters" (1:3, 6). Following each declaration by God, it happened. God had only to speak to make it so.

After each step of Creation, "God saw how good it was" (1:10, 12, 18, 21, 25). God is not only Creator, but also Evaluator. God did not create the world and walk away, but remains involved. God maintains a relationship with God's good creation after it is brought into being.

In Genesis 1, the Creation account is divided into days. The repeated phrase "There was evening and there was morning" divides the story into seven days (1:5, 8, 13, 19, 23, 31). The creation events are reported over six days, plus a day of rest.

Devotion

Take your Bible outside into God's creation. Take a moment to be still. Close your eyes and listen. What do you hear? Open your eyes and look around you. What do you see? Take a deep breath. What do you smell? Thank God for the beauty in the world around you. Marvel at the complexity of a spider's web or the melody of a bird's song. Turn to Psalm 8, and read the psalm as you stand or sit in the midst of God's good creation.

Whether this is your first time teaching or you have been teaching for years, thank you for doing God's work in this way.

biblestorybasics.com

BASIC _____

Plan

Bible Beginnings
Welcome
Picture the Bible Story
Bible Puzzle
Bible Play

Into the Bible
Time for the Bible Story
Open the Bible
Experience the Bible Story
Say the Bible Verse

Bible Connections
Animal Dance and Freeze
Abstract Creation Art

Live the Bible
I Can Take Care of God's
   Creation
Feed the Birds

Express Praise
Praise and Pray
Blessing

Bible Beginnings

Welcome

Supplies: Class Pack—Attendance Chart, p. 1; CD-ROM; CD player; tape; offering basket

• Display the attendance chart (Class Pack) and "Unit 1 Bible Verse Picture" (Class Pack—p. 1) at the children's eye level.

• Play "The B-I-B-L-E" from the CD-ROM (lyrics on p. 86) as you welcome each child.

• Have each child mark his or her attendance.

• Show the children where to place their offerings on the worship table.

SAY: Today, our Bible story is about Creation. A creation is something someone has made. The earth is God's creation. That means that God created the earth and everything in it.

• Point out the Bible verse picture, and say the Bible verse for the children.

Picture the Bible Story

Supplies: Leader Guide—p. 12, crayons or markers

• Photocopy "God Created the World" for each child.

• Give each child the picture.

ASK: What's in this picture?

SAY: This is a picture of how our earth looks from space. Pretend you are on a rocket ship flying through space far away from the earth. If you looked out your window, this is what the earth would look like.

• Encourage the children to decorate the picture with crayons or markers.

Bible Puzzle

Supplies: Bible Story Leaflets—Session 1, p. 4; star stickers, crayons, or markers

• Give each child a copy of today's Bible Story Leaflet.

• Encourage the children to add stars all around the earth. Give the children star stickers, or let the children add dots with crayons or markers to represent stars.

SAY: The Bible tells us that God created the earth, the sun, the moon, and the stars.

Bible Play

Supplies: green play dough, blue play dough

• Give each child a portion of green play dough and a portion of blue play dough.

• Encourage the children to mix the two colors together.

• Show the children how to form a ball with the play dough.

SAY: You've made the earth! The green is the land. The blue is the water. The Bible tells us that God created the earth and everything in it.

Into the Bible

Time for the Bible Story

SAY: Let's pretend that we are the earth spinning in space. Spin to our Story Area.

• Sing the following song to the tune of "She'll Be Coming 'Round the Mountain" as the children move. End the song in your large group area.

SING: Oh, our God made all the earth spin 'round the sun.
Oh, our God made all the earth spin 'round the sun.
Oh, our God made all the earth spin; oh, our God made all the earth spin;
Oh, our God made all the earth spin 'round the sun.

• Have the children sit down.

SAY: Today, our Bible story is about Creation. A creation is something someone has made. The earth is God's creation. That means that God created all the earth.

Open the Bible

Supplies: Bible Basics Storybook—pp. 12-13

• Tell the children the story "Creation."

Experience the Bible Story

Supplies: CEB Bible; Bible Story Leaflets—Session 1, pp. 2-3

• Show the children the Bible.

TODAY'S BIBLE TOOL: The Bible has two parts.

SAY: Our Bible has many stories. Some of the stories tell about the beginnings of God's people. These stories are in the Old Testament. Some of the stories tell about God's Son, Jesus. These stories are in the New Testament.

• Show the children the first chapter of Genesis.

SAY: Today, our story is the very first story in our Bible. It is chapter one in the Book of Genesis. Listen and watch as I tell the story. You can help me do some sounds and motions.

• Place the leaflet inside the Bible. Tell the children the story "Creation" from the leaflet, and encourage them to do the suggested sounds and motions with you.

Say the Bible Verse

Supplies: Class Pack—p. 1, Leader Guide—p. 88

• Show the children the Bible verse picture (Class Pack). Repeat the verse.

SAY: The word *supremely* means "very, very good."

• Teach the children signs in American Sign Language to go along with the verse (Leader Guide).

• Encourage the children to make the signs as they say the verse again.

Bible Connections

Animal Dance and Freeze

Supplies: CD-ROM, CD Player

• Have the children move to an open area of the room.

SAY: Today, our Bible story is about Creation. A creation is something someone has made. The earth is God's creation. That means that God created the earth and everything in it.

• Play "I've Got a River of Life" from the CD-ROM, and have the children dance around the room.

• Stop the music. Have the children freeze in place.

• Call one child by name.

ASK: What is your favorite animal? What sound does the animal make? How does the animal move?

• Play the music again, and have all the children move like that animal around the room.

• Continue playing the game until each child has had an opportunity to name an animal.

SAY: The Bible tells us that God made all the animals on the earth.

Abstract Creation Art

Supplies: plain paper or construction paper, crayons or markers

• Give each child a piece of paper.

• Place the crayons or markers where the children can reach them.

SAY: The Bible tells us that God made the earth and everything in it. We're going to use colors to help us remember the things God created. On day number one, God made the light. The light was called Day. What color is day? *(Find a yellow [or whichever color the children named] crayon or marker, and color on the paper.)* The dark was called Night. What color is night? *(Find a black [or whichever color the children named] crayon or marker, and color on your paper.)*

• Have each child pick out a day crayon or marker. Encourage the children to color with it anywhere on the paper. Then have each child pick out a night crayon or marker. Encourage the children to color with it anywhere on the paper.

• Continue explaining each day of Creation and letting the children suggest the corresponding color. Display the art in your room or in the hall.

Day	Creation	Suggested Color
Two	fluffy clouds	white
Three	land, seas, seeds	green, blue, brown
Four	sun, moon, stars	yellow, orange, white, silver
Five	fish, birds	red, orange, yellow, blue
Six	animals	brown, black, gray

Live the Bible

I Can Take Care of God's Creation

Supplies: none

• Say the following action poem, and lead the children in doing the motions.

I can take care of God's creation—
(Sweep your arms all around.)
The earth, the animals, and people too.
(Make a circle with your hands. Use your hands to make ears. Point to yourself.)

I can take care of God's creation.
(Sweep your arms all around.)
That's what God wants me to do.
(Touch both thumbs to your chest.)

So, growl like a bear, and fly like a bird.
(Make claws, and then flap your arms.)
Then hop, hop, hop like a kangaroo.
(Hop three times.)

I can take care of God's creation.
(Sweep your arms all around.)
That's what God wants me to do.
(Touch both thumbs to your chest.)

Feed the Birds

Supplies: chenille stems, O-shaped cereal, resealable plastic bags

SAY: One way we can help take care of God's creation is to feed the birds.

• Give each child a chenille stem with a knot or loop on one end.

• Show the children how to thread the O-shaped cereal onto their chenille stems.

• When a child's chenille stem is full, help the child fold over the end of the stem to keep the cereal from falling off. Place each bird treat inside a resealable plastic bag.

SAY: Take your bird treat home, and hang it outside where the birds can find it.

Express Praise

Praise and Pray

Supplies: CD-ROM, CD player

• Sing with the children the song "Hear Us As We Pray" from the CD-ROM (lyrics on p. 87). Encourage the children to name any prayer requests.

PRAY: Thank you, God, for all the wonderful things you have created. Amen.

Blessing

Supplies: Bible Story Leaflets—Parent Take-Home, Songbook Take-Home; child-safe mirror

• Hand one child in the circle the mirror. Have the child look into the mirror.

SAY: *(Child's name)* is part of God's good creation.

• Continue passing the mirror around the circle until you have blessed each child.

• Send home the "Using the Bible at Home" and "Bible Story Basics Songbook" with each child.

God Created the World

God saw everything he had made: it was supremely good. (Genesis 1:31)

Permission is granted to duplicate this page for local church use only. © 2019 Abingdon Press.

God's Image

Bible Verse: God saw everything he had made: it was supremely good. (Genesis 1:31)

Bible Story: Genesis 1:26–2:4a

Bible Background

Today's Bible story continues our study of Creation. Last week, we read up through the creation of land animals. Today, we learn about the last part of Creation—humans! The story presents us a hymn of celebration. Humans are the magnificent completion of God's universe.

Scholars and theologians have spent lots of time discussing what it means to be made in the image of God. Christian interpreters thought that to be made in the image of God meant that we were made into spiritual beings, meaning we have souls, while other creations do not. Some modern scholars believe being created in God's image means that we all have divine worth and should all be treated with equal respect. Still, other scholars point to the language. The word *image* comes from the same root word as *imagination*. They conclude that our ability to imagine and be creative is part of how we're made in the image of God.

More recent biblical scholars have looked at ancient cultures around Israel to understand the idea of being created in the image of God. Area kings were described as representations of their gods. With this understanding, Genesis writers identify that humans are representatives of God on earth.

The end of the Creation hymn states that we, as representatives of God on earth, have a responsibility to care for the earth. Being made in the image of God is a hefty responsibility to love and care for all creation.

Help your children expand their love for God's creation. Talk about the beautiful things they see. Ask questions to help them become aware of the world around them. Discuss ways they can help take care of the world: recycling, conserving water, turning off lights when leaving a room, adopting and caring for a pet, and cleaning up trash. These simple tasks can help children begin to realize they are part of a big world and have a responsibility to respect and care for it.

Devotion

Look in a mirror and say three things you like about the way you look. Then say three things you like about the way you act. After each thing, say, "I am made in the image of God." Read Psalm 100. After reading the entire psalm, read Psalm 100:3 out loud.

biblestorybasics.com

BASIC

Plan

Bible Beginnings
Welcome
Picture the Bible Story
Bible Puzzle
Bible Play

Into the Bible
Time for the Bible Story
Open the Bible
Experience the Bible Story
Say the Bible Verse

Bible Connections
God Made Me
Thumb-body Special

Live the Bible
Taking Care
A Day of Rest

Express Praise
Praise and Pray
Blessing

Bible Beginnings

Welcome

Supplies: Class Pack—Attendance Chart, p. 1; CD-ROM; CD player; tape; offering basket

• Display the attendance chart (Class Pack) and "Unit 1 Bible Verse Picture" (Class Pack—p. 1) at the children's eye level.

• Play "The B-I-B-L-E" from the CD-ROM (lyrics on p. 86) as you welcome each child.

• Have each child mark his or her attendance.

• Show the children where to place their offerings on the worship table.

SAY: Today, our Bible story is about what God created on the sixth day of Creation. We know God made the earth and the sky; all the plants and trees; the sun, moon, and stars; and all the fish, birds, and animals.

ASK: Can you think of anything else God made?

SAY: God made people!

• Point out the Bible verse picture, and say the Bible verse for the children.

Picture the Bible Story

Supplies: Leader Guide—p. 18, crayons or markers

• Photocopy "God Created People" for each child.

• Give each child the picture.

ASK: What's in this picture? Do they all look alike?

SAY: God created people in all shapes and sizes, and God loves them all.

• Encourage the children to decorate the picture with crayons or markers.

Bible Puzzle

Supplies: Bible Story Leaflets—Session 2, p. 4; crayons or markers

• Give each child a copy of today's Bible Story Leaflet.

• Encourage each child to decorate the face to look like himself or herself.

SAY: The Bible tells us that God made people. That means God made each one of you. Each person is special. Each person is different.

Bible Play

Supplies: play dough, gingerbread person cookie cutters

• Give each child a portion of play dough.

• Encourage the children to use the cookie cutters with the dough. If you don't have cookie cutters, let the children form their own people out of the dough.

SAY: Today, our Bible story is about what happened on the sixth day of Creation. God created people. Each person is special. Each person is different.

Into the Bible

Time for the Bible Story

SAY: God made each one of us different. Let's play a game about us. If what I say is true about you, move to our Story Area. If you wear glasses, take giant steps to our Story Area. If you like pizza, hop to our Story Area. If you have blue eyes, walk backwards to our Story Area. If you are a boy, twirl to our Story Area. If you are a girl, gallop to our Story Area.

• Have the children sit down.

SAY: God loves all people.

Open the Bible

Supplies: Bible Basics Storybook—pp. 14-15

• Tell the children the story "God's Image."

Experience the Bible Story

Supplies: CEB Bible; Bible Story Leaflets—Session 2, pp. 2-3

• Show the children the Bible.

TODAY'S BIBLE TOOL: The Bible has two parts. The two parts are divided into books.

SAY: Our Bible has two parts: the Old Testament and the New Testament. The two parts are divided into books.

• Show the children a book in the Old Testament and a book in the New Testament.

SAY: Today, our story is from the first book in our Bible, the Book of Genesis. The word *genesis* means "beginning." We are learning about all the good things God created at the beginning of the earth. Listen and watch as I tell the story. You can help me do some motions.

• Place the leaflet inside the Bible. Tell the children the story "God's Image" from the leaflet, and encourage them to do the suggested motions with you.

ASK: How does it make you feel to know that God created you? that God loves you?

Say the Bible Verse

Supplies: Class Pack—p. 1, Leader Guide—p. 88

• Show the children the Bible verse picture (Class Pack). Repeat the verse.

SAY: The word *supremely* means "very, very good."

• Teach the children signs in American Sign Language to go along with the verse (Leader Guide).

• Encourage the children to make the signs as they say the verse again.

Bible Connections

God Made Me

Supplies: none

• Have the children move to an open area of the room.

• Say the poem printed below. Point to your body as indicated in the poem. Have the children say the missing word and point to their own bodies.

> Look at me, look at me; I am special, as you can see.
> I have one _____. *(Point to your nose.)* It's on my face.
> I have two _____ *(Point to your legs.)* to run a race.
> I have two _____ *(Point to your ears.)* to hear you talk.
> I have two _____ *(Point to your feet.)* to take a walk.
> I have two _____ *(Point to your eyes.)* to see the sky.
> I have two _____ *(Point to your hands.)* to wave goodbye.
> Look at me, look at me; I am special, 'cause God made me!

Thumb-body Special

Supplies: magnifying glass, plain paper, washable markers, wet wipes

SAY: The Bible tells us that God created people. Each person is special. Each person is different.

• Have the children look at their fingertips.

SAY: Look at the tiny lines on the tips of your fingers. Those lines make up your fingerprints. You are the only person in the whole world who has your fingerprints.

• Let the children take turns looking at their fingerprints through the magnifying glass.

• Give each child a piece of paper. Show each child how to use a washable marker to color the pad of his or her thumb and then to press the colored thumb on the paper. Encourage each child to make several thumbprints.

• Have the children use wet wipes to remove the marker from their thumbs.

SAY: I'm so glad that God made you just the way you are!

Live the Bible

Taking Care

Supplies: a variety of dolls and stuffed animals; plastic doctor kit supplies, such as stethoscopes, thermometers, and bandages

• Invite each child to choose a doll or stuffed animal to take care of. Encourage each child to pretend to check his or her doll's or animal's heartbeat, feed it, take its temperature, bandage it up, and rock it to sleep.

SAY: The Bible tells us God wanted people to take care of creation. One way we can take care of creation is by taking care of babies and animals.

A Day of Rest

Supplies: construction paper or newsprint, crayons or markers

SAY: The Bible tells us God created the earth. Let's remember what God created.

• Have the children name things God created.

SAY: The Bible says that "God saw everything he had made: it was supremely good." That's our Bible verse. Let's say it together.

• Repeat the Bible verse with the children.

SAY: When God was finished, the Bible tells us that God did something important. God rested. We call the day God rested the Sabbath. It is a special day to rest and worship God. Let's make mats to use as we rest on the Sabbath.

• Give each child a large piece of construction paper or newsprint.

• Let the children decorate the paper with crayons or markers.

• Have the children take their mats to an open area of the room and lie down.

• Sing the following song to the tune of "God Is So Good" as the children quietly lie down on their mats.

SING: God saw the earth.
God saw the earth.
God saw the earth
Was supremely good.

Express Praise

Praise and Pray

Supplies: CD-ROM, CD player

• Sing with the children the song "Hear Us As We Pray" from the CD-ROM (lyrics on p. 87). Encourage the children to name any prayer requests.

PRAY: Thank you, God, for all the wonderful things you have created. Amen.

Blessing

Supplies: child-safe mirror

• Hand one child in the circle the mirror. Have the child look into the mirror.

SAY: (Child's name) is part of God's good creation.

• Continue passing the mirror around the circle until you have blessed each child.

God Created People

God saw everything he had made: it was supremely good. (Genesis 1:31)

Permission is granted to duplicate this page for local church use only. © 2019 Abingdon Press.

Adam and Eve

Bible Verse: God saw everything he had made: it was supremely good. (Genesis 1:31)

Bible Story: Genesis 2:4b–3:24

biblestorybasics.com

Bible Background

Today's Bible story is the second account of Creation, the story of Adam and Eve and the tree of life in the middle of the garden of Eden. The first story (Genesis 1:1–2:4a) culminates with the creation of human beings as one act (1:27) and the directive for humans to have dominion over all God created. In the second Creation story (2:4b–3:24), the creation of humankind happens in two stages, but it is not complete until man and woman stand in partnership with each other.

The story that includes Adam and Eve and the garden of Eden is a colorful story, filled with rich, memorable images—Adam's formation from the dust of the earth, Eve's creation from one of Adam's ribs, a magnificent garden of delights, a tree of life, a wily serpent, and angels with a fiery sword. Through these stories, the Hebrew people tried to answer some of their most basic questions: Why do human beings, created in the image of God, refuse to acknowledge the sovereignty of their Creator? How did evil come into such a perfect creation?

God created human beings with a special relationship to God and one another. But those human beings also were given a gift that no other living creature was given—the ability to choose between right and wrong. Adam and Eve made the choice to eat from the tree in the middle of the garden. Through this act, human beings learned that along with this freedom to choose came the consequences of those choices.

For young children, the two biblical accounts of Creation flow into one story. It is not necessary at their age to make a distinction between the two stories. The children will enjoy imagining Adam giving names to the animals. Talk about some of the funny names that animals have, like *hippopotamus*, *cockatoo*, and other names. Remind the children that their parents chose names for them.

Devotion

Think about a time when you made a mistake or a bad choice—what were the consequences? Where was God in that situation? How did God redeem it? There are many examples of people in the Bible who made mistakes, such as David, Jonah, the woman at the well, and Peter; yet God was able to use these people to complete God's purpose. Read Psalm 103:12-14. How does it feel to know God forgives our bad choices?

Bible Beginnings

Welcome

Supplies: Class Pack—Attendance Chart, p. 1; CD-ROM; CD player; tape; offering basket

• Display the attendance chart (Class Pack) and "Unit 1 Bible Verse Picture" (Class Pack—p. 1) at the children's eye level.

• Play "The B-I-B-L-E" from the CD-ROM (lyrics on p. 86) as you welcome each child.

• Have each child mark his or her attendance.

• Show the children where to place their offerings on the worship table.

SAY: The Bible tells us that God made the first people and named them Adam and Eve.

• Point out the Bible verse picture, and say the Bible verse for the children.

Picture the Bible Story

Supplies: Leader Guide—p. 24, crayons or markers

• Photocopy "Adam and Eve in the Garden" for each child.

• Give each child the picture.

SAY: The Bible tells us that God made Adam and Eve. Adam and Eve lived in a beautiful garden.

• Encourage the children to decorate the picture with crayons or markers.

Bible Puzzle

Supplies: Bible Story Leaflets—Session 3, p. 4; crayons or markers

• Give each child a copy of today's Bible Story Leaflet.

• Encourage the children to find a crescent moon, a star, a flower, a sprouting tree with one tiny leaf, and an acorn hidden in the picture.

SAY: The Bible tells us that God made Adam and Eve. Adam and Eve lived in a beautiful garden. It was a garden where God had planted all kinds of plants and trees, and there was a pretty river watering the garden.

Bible Play

Supplies: play dough, plastic or silk flowers and plants, small plastic animals

• Give each child a portion of play dough.

• Encourage the children to flatten out their play dough to make the ground.

• Show the children how to stick the flowers and plants in the play dough to make a garden.

• Let the children add the plastic animals among the flowers and plants.

SAY: God made a beautiful garden for Adam and Eve. It was a garden with all kinds of plants and trees. God also made all kinds of animals to live in the garden with Adam and Eve. God even let Adam name the animals!

Into the Bible

Time for the Bible Story

SAY: Let's pretend that we are animals in the garden with Adam and Eve. Think of an animal you want to be. Move like that animal to our Story Area.

• Encourage the children to move like the animal they chose to be.

• Have the children sit down.

ASK: What animal are you? What's your name?

Open the Bible

Supplies: Bible Basics Storybook—pp. 16-17

• Tell the children the story "Adam and Eve."

Experience the Bible Story

Supplies: CEB Bible; Bible Story Leaflets—Session 3, pp. 2-3

• Show the children the Bible.

TODAY'S BIBLE TOOL: Genesis is the first book in the Bible.

SAY: Our Bible has two parts: the Old Testament and the New Testament. The two parts are divided into books.

• Show the children a book in the Old Testament and a book in the New Testament.

SAY: Today, our story is from the first book in our Bible, the Book of Genesis. The word *genesis* means "beginning." We are learning about all the good things God created at the beginning of the earth. Listen and watch as I tell the story. You can help me do some sounds and motions.

• Place the leaflet inside the Bible. Tell the children the story "Adam and Eve" from the leaflet, and encourage them to do the suggested sounds and motions with you.

Say the Bible Verse

Supplies: Class Pack—p. 1, Leader Guide—p. 88, CD-ROM, CD player, stuffed animal

• Show the children the Bible verse picture (Class Pack). Repeat the verse.

• Teach the children signs in American Sign Language to go along with the verse (Leader Guide).

• Encourage the children to make the signs as they say the verse again.

• Have the children sit in a circle. Hand one child in the circle a stuffed animal.

• Play "The B-I-B-L-E" from the CD-ROM, and have the children pass the animal.

• Stop the music. Have the child holding the stuffed animal stand up.

• While the child is standing, have everyone say the Bible verse together.

• Continue the game until everyone has stood up while holding the stuffed animal.

Bible Connections

Ring Around the Garden

Supplies: none

• Have the children move to an open area of the room.

• Have the children stand in a circle and hold hands.

SAY: The Bible tells us that God made the first people and named them Adam and Eve.

• Have the children walk around in a circle as you say the following action poem. You can also sing the poem to the tune of "Ring Around the Rosie."

So, God made the first man,
(Walk around the circle.)
The first man, the first man.
So, God made the first man,
And Adam was his name.
(All fall down.)

Then God made a garden,
(Walk around the circle.)
A garden, a garden.

Then God made a garden,
And Eden was its name.
(All fall down.)

Then God made a woman,
(Walk around the circle.)
A woman, a woman.
Then God made a woman,
And Eve was her name.
(All fall down.)

The Special Tree

Supplies: Leader Guide—p. 91, crayons or markers, colored construction paper, glue

• Photocopy "The Special Tree" for each child.

SAY: The Bible tells us that God made a special tree that grew in the middle of the garden. God told Adam and Eve that they could not eat the fruit from this tree. Let's make pictures of the special tree.

• Give each child the picture.

• Let the children decorate the tree trunk with crayons or markers.

• Show each child how to tear the colored construction paper into very small pieces.

• Have the children glue the pieces of construction paper onto the tree branches to make leaves and flowers.

SAY: Adam and Eve chose to eat the fruit from the special tree. Because Adam and Eve chose to disobey God, they had to leave the beautiful garden, but God still loved and cared for Adam and Eve after they left the garden.

Live the Bible

Plant a Garden

Supplies: plastic table covering, paper cups, spoons, potting soil, grass seeds, watering can, water

• Cover the table with the covering.

- Help each child spoon potting soil into a cup, and show each child how to poke seeds down into the soil. Add a layer of potting soil on top of the seeds, and then let the children water their cup gardens with the watering can.

SAY: Your cup garden can remind you of the story of Adam and Eve and the garden.

Make a Choice

Supplies: none

SAY: Adam and Eve made the choice to disobey God. We make choices every day. Sometimes we make good choices. Sometimes we make bad choices. Listen as I read some short stories. If you think the children in the story made a good choice, hold your thumbs up. If you think the children made a bad choice, hold your thumbs down.

Mother told Ginny she could not eat any cookies before dinner, but Ginny ran into the kitchen and grabbed a cookie. *(Hold your thumbs down.)* Mother told Ginny she could not eat any cookies before dinner, so Ginny looked at her books until dinner time. *(Hold your thumbs up.)*

Ben and Lucas both wanted to watch television. Ben wanted to watch a cartoon about superheroes. Lucas wanted to watch a movie about a dog. "Go ahead and watch your cartoon," said Lucas to Ben. "We can watch the movie when the cartoon is over." *(Hold your thumbs up.)* Ben and Lucas both wanted to watch television. They argued and argued until their mother turned off the television and sent the boys to their rooms. *(Hold your thumbs down.)*

Gavin and Josie were playing with play dough. They divided the dough in half, so they both had enough to make lots of animals. *(Hold your thumbs up.)* Gavin and Josie were playing with play dough. Gavin grabbed all the blue dough and wouldn't give any to Josie. *(Hold your thumbs down.)*

SAY: God loved Adam and Eve even though they made a bad choice. God loves us.

Express Praise

Praise and Pray

Supplies: CD-ROM, CD player

- Sing with the children the song "Hear Us As We Pray" from the CD-ROM (lyrics on p. 87). Encourage the children to name any prayer requests.

PRAY: Thank you, God, for all the wonderful things you have created. Amen.

Blessing

Supplies: child-safe mirror

- Hand one child in the circle the mirror. Have the child look into the mirror.

SAY: *(Child's name)* is part of God's good creation.

- Continue passing the mirror around the circle until you have blessed each child.

Adam and Eve in the Garden

God saw everything he had made: it was supremely good. (Genesis 1:31)

Permission is granted to duplicate this page for local church use only. © 2019 Abingdon Press.

Noah

Bible Verse: God saw everything he had made: it was supremely good. (Genesis 1:31)

Bible Story: Genesis 6:1–9:17

Bible Background

After the creation of humanity, God declared it "supremely good" (Genesis 1:31). Just five chapters later, God "regretted making human beings on the earth, and he was heartbroken" (6:6). God decided to destroy this part of creation. But there was Noah, who still walked with God. So, when God decided to destroy humanity, Noah and his family were spared.

God told Noah to build an ark. Unlike some biblical figures, such as Moses, who negotiated and argued with God, Noah didn't interact with God's pronouncement. Noah had to decide, however, whether to trust God enough to follow God's instructions. "Noah did everything exactly as God commanded him" (6:22). This included gathering pairs of animals and enough food to feed the animals and his family.

After the Flood, God made a promise to Noah and every living creature that there never again will be a flood to destroy the earth. God's covenant indicated God's commitment to the future of a less-than-perfect world. Even though human beings have faults, God continues to place confidence in them.

God uses the rainbow to mark the covenant established with Noah and all living creatures. The rainbow serves as a reminder to God of God's commitment to humankind (9:14-15). The rainbow also reminds God's people of God's constant and never-ending faithfulness.

As you tell the story of Noah to your pre-readers, don't dwell on the destruction of the world. Focus instead on Noah's faithfulness and how God cared for Noah, Noah's family, and the animals. With this focus, the rainbow becomes a reminder of God's promise to care for all of us.

Devotion

Have you ever made a promise to someone? A promise is like a covenant. God made a covenant with Noah after the flood. Read Genesis 9:8-17. The rainbow is a symbol of the covenant between God and the earth. It is a covenant that reaches from the time of Noah to future generations. It is a covenant that brings us hope. When you see a rainbow, remember God's promise.

biblestorybasics.com

BASIC

Plan

Bible Beginnings
Welcome
Picture the Bible Story
Bible Puzzle
Bible Play

Into the Bible
Time for the Bible Story
Open the Bible
Experience the Bible Story
Say the Bible Verse

Bible Connections
Animals on the Ark
Rainbow Romp

Live the Bible
Make Your Own Rainbow
Rainbow Mural

Express Praise
Praise and Pray
Blessing

Bible Beginnings

Welcome

Supplies: Class Pack—Attendance Chart, p. 1; CD-ROM; CD player; tape; offering basket

- Display the attendance chart (Class Pack) and "Unit 1 Bible Verse Picture" (Class Pack—p. 1) at the children's eye level.

- Play "The B-I-B-L-E" from the CD-ROM (lyrics on p. 86) as you welcome each child.

- Have each child mark his or her attendance.

- Show the children where to place their offerings on the worship table.

SAY: Today, our Bible story is about a man named Noah. Our story about Noah has a big boat, lots of animals, and a rainbow. Noah trusted God.

- Point out the Bible verse picture, and say the Bible verse for the children.

Picture the Bible Story

Supplies: Leader Guide—p. 30, crayons or markers

- Photocopy "Noah's Ark" for each child.

- Give each child the picture.

SAY: Today, our Bible story is about a man named Noah. God told Noah to build a big boat. The boat is called an ark. God told Noah to bring two of every animal onto the ark. Noah trusted God and did what God told him to do.

- Encourage the children to decorate the picture with crayons or markers.

- Invite the children to find and circle the lions, the penguins, the giraffes, and the elephants in the picture.

Bible Puzzle

Supplies: Bible Story Leaflets—Session 4, p. 4; crayons or markers

- Give each child a copy of today's Bible Story Leaflet.

- Encourage the children to match each animal with the food the animal eats.

ASK: How much food do you think Noah had to put on the ark?

Bible Play

Supplies: red, orange, yellow, green, blue, indigo, and violet play dough

- Let the children enjoy the different colors of play dough.

ASK: Where do we see rainbows? What colors are in rainbows?

SAY: God told Noah to build a really big boat. God told Noah to bring animals and his family onto the boat. Then it rained and rained. It rained so hard the boat began to float, but Noah, his family, and the animals were safe on the boat. After the rain stopped, God placed a rainbow in the sky. The rainbow helped Noah and his family remember that God promised to take care of them. When we see a rainbow, we can remember that God loves us and promises to take care of us.

Into the Bible

Time for the Bible Story

SAY: God put a rainbow in the sky to help Noah and his family remember God's promise to take care of the earth. Let's wave our arms in the air like a rainbow as we move to our Story Area.

• Sing the following song to the tune of "Mary Had a Little Lamb" as the children move. End the song in your large group area.

SING: See the rainbow in the sky, in the sky, in the sky.
See the rainbow in the sky, with colors bright and true.
God put the rainbow in the sky, in the sky, in the sky.
God put the rainbow in the sky, with colors bright and true.

• Have the children sit down.

Open the Bible

Supplies: Bible Basics Storybook—pp. 18-19

• Tell the children the story "Noah."

Experience the Bible Story

Supplies: CEB Bible; Bible Story Leaflets—Session 4, pp. 2-3

• Show the children the Bible.

TODAY'S BIBLE TOOL: Genesis is the first book of the Bible. Genesis has chapters that tell us different stories.

SAY: Our Bible has two parts: the Old Testament and the New Testament. The two parts are divided into books.

• Show the children a book in the Old Testament and a book in the New Testament.

SAY: Today, our story is from the first book in our Bible, the Book of Genesis. The Book of Genesis is divided into chapters. The story of the Creation is in chapter one. Today, our story begins in chapter six. Listen and watch as I tell the story. You can help me do some motions.

• Place the leaflet inside the Bible. Tell the children the story "Noah" from the leaflet, and encourage them to do the suggested motions with you.

ASK: How do you think Noah and his family felt when they saw the rainbow?

Say the Bible Verse

Supplies: Class Pack—p. 1, Leader Guide—p. 88

• Show the children the Bible verse picture (Class Pack). Repeat the verse.

• Teach the children signs in American Sign Language to go along with the verse (Leader Guide).

• Encourage the children to make the signs as they say the verse again.

Bible Connections

Animals on the Ark

Supplies: none

• Have the children stand in a circle in an open area of the room.

• Say the following action poem, and encourage the children to make the sounds and do the motions described in the poem. You can also sing the poem to the tune of "The Wheels on the Bus."

The cows on the ark say,
"Moo, moo, moo,
Moo, moo, moo,
Moo, moo, moo."
The cows on the ark say,
"Moo, moo, moo,"
Walking side by side.

The bunnies on the ark go
Hop, hop, hop,
Hop, hop, hop,
Hop, hop, hop.
The bunnies on the ark go
Hop, hop, hop,
Hopping side by side.

The ducks on the ark say,
"Quack, quack, quack,
Quack, quack, quack,
Quack, quack, quack."
The ducks on the ark say,
"Quack, quack, quack,"
Waddling side by side.

The bees on the ark go,
"Buzz, buzz, buzz,
Buzz, buzz, buzz,
Buzz, buzz, buzz."
The bees on the ark go,
"Buzz, buzz, buzz,"
Flying side by side.

Rainbow Romp

Supplies: CD-ROM; CD player; red, orange, yellow, green, blue, indigo, and violet crepe paper streamers or ribbons; tape

• Cut the crepe paper streamers or ribbons into 12-inch strips.

• Gather a strip in each of the available colors. Wrap tape around one of the ends of the strips to make a rainbow streamer. Make a streamer for each child.

• Give each child a rainbow streamer, and have the children stand in an open area of the room.

• Play "The B-I-B-L-E" from the CD-ROM, and let the children dance and wave their streamers as the music plays.

SAY: God told Noah to build a really big boat. God told Noah to bring animals and his family onto the boat. Then it rained and rained. It rained so hard the boat began to float, but Noah, his family, and the animals were safe on the boat. After the rain stopped, God placed a rainbow in the sky. The rainbow helped Noah and his family remember that God promised to take care of the earth.

Live the Bible

Make Your Own Rainbow

Supplies: white paper, scissors, flashlight, tape, clear glass container, water

• Fold a piece of white paper in half. Fold the paper in half again. Cut a triangle from the corner where the two folded edges meet. This will make a hole in the center of your paper.

• Fit a flashlight into the hole made in the paper. Secure the paper to the flashlight with tape.

SAY: When we see a rainbow, we can remember that God loves us and promises to take care of us.

• Fill a clear glass container with water, and hold the flashlight and paper above the container so that the light shines directly on the water.

• Watch the rainbow appear on the surface surrounding the glass container. You may need to turn off the lights to make the rainbow more visible.

• Let each child have a turn holding the flashlight and making a rainbow.

Rainbow Mural

Supplies: large sheet of paper, marker, scraps of construction paper, glue

• Lay the large sheet of paper on a table. Draw a rainbow shape on the paper with a marker.

• Encourage the children to glue the construction paper to the rainbow shape.

SAY: When we see a rainbow, we can remember that God loves us and promises to take care of us.

Express Praise

Praise and Pray

Supplies: CD-ROM, CD player

• Sing with the children the song "Hear Us As We Pray" from the CD-ROM (lyrics on p. 87). Encourage the children to name any prayer requests.

PRAY: Thank you, God, for all the wonderful things you have created. Amen.

Blessing

Supplies: child-safe mirror

• Hand one child in the circle the mirror. Have the child look into the mirror.

SAY: (Child's name) is part of God's good creation.

• Continue passing the mirror around the circle until you have blessed each child.

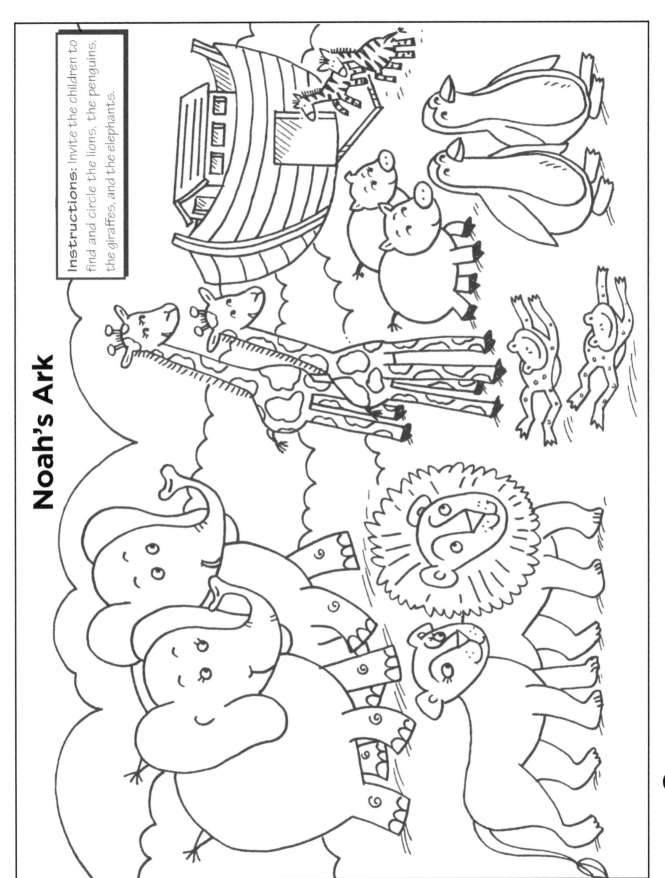

Noah's Ark

Instructions: Invite the children to find and circle the lions, the penguins, the giraffes, and the elephants.

God saw everything he had made: it was supremely good. (Genesis 1:31)

Permission is granted to duplicate this page for local church use only. © 2019 Abingdon Press.

Tower of Babel

Bible Verse: God saw everything he had made: it was supremely good. (Genesis 1:31)

Bible Story: Genesis 11:1-9

biblestorybasics.com

Bible Background

The story of the tower of Babel is the last story in the section of Genesis that deals with the universal scope of God's creation. The first 11 chapters deal with the origin and history of humanity as a whole. The chapters include the creation of the world, the worldwide flood, and the repopulation of the world through the descendants of Noah.

Historically, people have read the story of the tower of Babel as a story of God's punishment. In this reading, the humans who began constructing the tower were excessively proud, competing with God and trying to make a name for themselves. God thwarted this display of human pride by diversifying the languages and scattering the people across the earth.

There is another way to read the story, however, that has existed throughout Judeo-Christian tradition and reemerged in biblical scholarship. Commentators recognized that the ending of the story—that people were dispersed all over the earth—echoes God's command at the beginning of Genesis for humans to multiply and fill the earth. But after surviving the flood, these people wanted to stay together, not set out and discover new worlds.

Their wish was in conflict with God's desire to create a new world with different cultures. "Therefore, it is named Babel, because there the LORD mixed up the language of all the earth; and from there the LORD dispersed them over all the earth" (11:9). God forced the people to spread out, create new cultures, and explore new places. God's vision for a diverse humanity that spread throughout the world was accomplished.

Devotion

Today's session invites you to appreciate diversity. Because our world is increasingly interconnected, being open is important. This week, do something to learn about people who are different from you. You might go to a local ethnic festival or restaurant. You might go to the library and look at books about other cultures. Find music from different cultures on the Internet. After each experience, thank God for a world filled with beautiful differences.

BASIC

Plan

Bible Beginnings
Welcome
Picture the Bible Story
Bible Puzzle
Bible Play

Into the Bible
Time for the Bible Story
Open the Bible
Experience the Bible Story
Say the Bible Verse

Bible Connections
Build a Tower
Tower Rhymes

Live the Bible
Graph Your Class
Bible Verse Review

Express Praise
Praise and Pray
Blessing

Bible Beginnings

Welcome

Supplies: Class Pack—Attendance Chart, p. 1; CD-ROM; CD player; tape; offering basket

• Display the attendance chart (Class Pack) and "Unit 1 Bible Verse Picture" (Class Pack—p. 1) at the children's eye level.

• Play "The B-I-B-L-E" from the CD-ROM (lyrics on p. 86) as you welcome each child.

• Have each child mark his or her attendance.

• Show the children where to place their offerings on the worship table.

SAY: The people in our Bible story today wanted to live and work together in one place. They decided to work together to build a tall tower. But the people forgot something very important. They forgot to listen to God. God wanted them to live in different places. They did not do what God wanted them to do.

• Point out the Bible verse picture, and say the Bible verse for the children.

Picture the Bible Story

Supplies: Leader Guide—p. 36, crayons or markers, cotton balls, glue

• Photocopy "The Tall Tower" for each child.

• Give each child the picture.

SAY: The people in our Bible story worked together to build a tall tower. They wanted the tower to reach high into the sky.

• Encourage the children to decorate the picture with crayons or markers.

• Show the children how to make cotton balls wispy by stretching them. Then have the children glue wispy cotton balls around the top of the tower to represent clouds.

SAY: The people forgot something very important. They forgot to listen to God. God wanted them to live in different places. They did not do what God wanted them to do. We'll find out what happened to them when we hear our Bible story.

Bible Puzzle

Supplies: Bible Story Leaflets—Session 5, p. 4; crayons or markers

• Give each child a copy of today's Bible Story Leaflet.

• Encourage the children to match each child with the correct shadow.

SAY: In today's Bible story, we'll learn that God wanted people to be different.

Bible Play

Supplies: play dough

• Encourage the children to make bricks with the play dough. Then encourage the children to build towers with their bricks.

SAY: The people in our Bible story worked together to build a tall tower. They wanted the tower to reach high into the sky.

Into the Bible

Time for the Bible Story

SAY: Our Bible story is about a tall tower. Let's pretend that we're building a tall tower.

• Have the children stretch their arms overhead and stand on their tiptoes.

SAY: The people in our Bible story wanted to build a tower all the way to the sky. Let's sing a song about the tower while we move to our Story Area.

• Sing the following song to the tune of "This Is the Way" as the children move. End the song in your large group area.

SING: This is the way we build a tower, build a tower, build a tower.
    This the way we build a tower, stretching to the sky.

• Have the children sit down.

Open the Bible

Supplies: Bible Basics Storybook—pp. 20-21

• Tell the children the story "Tower of Babel."

Experience the Bible Story

Supplies: CEB Bible; Bible Story Leaflets—Session 5, pp. 2-3

• Show the children the Bible.

TODAY'S BIBLE TOOL: The first books of the Bible are in the Old Testament.

SAY: Our Bible has many stories. Some of the stories tell about the beginnings of God's people. These stories are in the Old Testament. Some of the stories tell about God's Son, Jesus. These stories are in the New Testament.

• Show the children Genesis 11.

SAY: Today, our story is in the first book of the Bible. The first books of the Bible are in the Old Testament. Listen and watch as I tell the story. You can help me do some sounds and motions.

• Place the leaflet inside the Bible. Tell the children the story "Tower of Babel" from the leaflet, and encourage them to say the words printed in bold and do the suggested motions with you.

ASK: Do you know a word in a different language? What is it?

Say the Bible Verse

Supplies: Class Pack—p. 1, Leader Guide—p. 88

• Show the children the Bible verse picture (Class Pack). Repeat the verse.

• Teach the children signs in American Sign Language to go along with the verse (Leader Guide).

• Encourage the children to make the signs as they say the verse again.

Bible Connections

Build a Tower

Supplies: paper bags, newsprint or recycled paper, masking tape

SAY: The people in our Bible story today wanted to live and work together in one place. They decided to work together to build a tall tower out of bricks. Let's make some bricks out of paper bags.

• Show the children how to crumple sheets of newsprint or recycled paper and stuff the paper inside the bags. Fold over the top of the bags, and seal the bags shut with masking tape.

• Encourage the children to use the bricks to build a tower on the floor.

SAY: The people building the tower forgot to listen to God. They did not do what God wanted them to do, so God mixed up their languages. The people could not work together because they could not understand each other. The people left the tower and went to live in different places all over the earth.

• Let the children knock the tower down.

Tower Rhymes

Supplies: none

• Have the children move to an open area of the room.

SAY: Our Bible story is about a tall tower. Let's pretend that we are climbing a tower.

• Have the children pretend to climb up a tower.

SAY: Now stand still. When I call your name, do what I tell you to do.

• Call each child by name, and tell him or her how to move. If you have a large group of children, call more than one child at a time.

(Child's name), **climb up the tower;** touch the floor.
Now go ahead: hop to the door.

(Child's name), **climb up the tower;** turn around.
Now sit right down on the ground.

(Child's name), **climb up the tower;** touch your nose.
Now let's see you tap your toes.

(Child's name), **climb up the tower;** jump up high.
Clap your hands and wave goodbye.

(Child's name), **climb up the tower;** tap your knees.
Now shake each foot, if you please.

(Child's name), **climb up the tower;** blink your eyes.
Now raise your hands up to the skies.

(Child's name), **climb up the tower;** stand up tall.
Now tiptoe 'til you touch a wall.

SAY: The people building the tower forgot to listen to God. God wanted them to live in different places. They did not do what God wanted them to do, so God mixed up their languages. Now the people could not work together because they could not understand each other. The people left the tower and went to live in different places all over the earth.

Live the Bible

Graph Your Class

Supplies: posterboard, marker, stickers

• Use the marker to make seven columns across the posterboard. Label the columns "Brown Hair," "Blonde Hair," "Red Hair," "Brown Eyes," "Blue Eyes," "Green Eyes," and "Hazel Eyes."

• Show the children the graph.

ASK: Who has brown hair?

• Give each child with brown hair a sticker. Have each child with brown hair place the sticker in the column marked "Brown Hair." Repeat this for each column. Once you are finished, count the stickers in each column.

SAY: Each of us has some things that are the same, and each of us has some things that are different. God wanted people to be different.

Bible Verse Review

Supplies: ball

• Have the children sit in a circle on the floor. Tell the children to spread their legs in a V shape pointing toward the center of the circle. Sit in the circle with the children.

• Roll the ball to a child in the circle.

SAY: (Child's name), you are made in God's image. "God saw everything he made: it was supremely good" (Genesis 1:31).

• Have the child repeat the Bible verse and then roll the ball back to you. Continue until you have rolled the ball to every child.

Express Praise

Praise and Pray

Supplies: CD-ROM, CD player

• Sing with the children the song "Hear Us As We Pray" from the CD-ROM (lyrics on p. 87). Encourage the children to name any prayer requests.

PRAY: Thank you, God, for all the wonderful things you have created. Amen.

Blessing

Supplies: child-safe mirror

• Hand one child in the circle the mirror. Have the child look into the mirror.

SAY: (Child's name) is part of God's good creation.

• Continue passing the mirror around the circle until you have blessed each child.

The Tall Tower

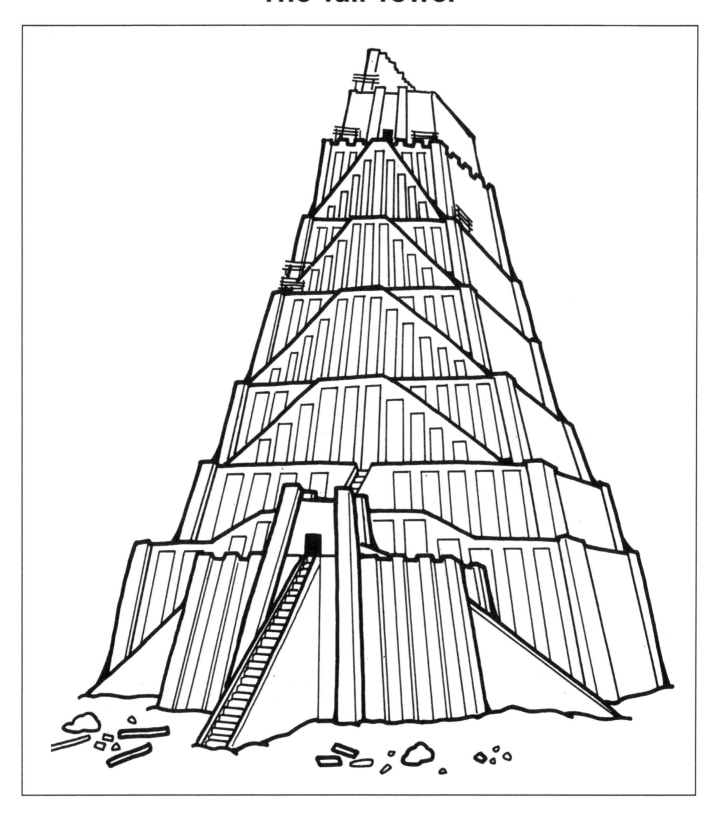

God saw everything he had made: it was supremely good. (Genesis 1:31)

Permission is granted to duplicate this page for local church use only. © 2019 Abingdon Press.

Abraham and Sarah

Bible Verse: Look up at the sky and count the stars... This is how many children you will have. (Genesis 15:5)

Bible Story: Genesis 12:1-9; 15:1-6

Bible Background

Today's Bible story is sometimes considered to be the beginning of the story of God's people. God appeared to Abraham and told him to pack up his family and belongings and travel to a land God would show him. This move was a continuation of a journey begun by Abraham's family years earlier. Abraham's family left their home in Ur of the Chaldeans to travel to Canaan. Abraham's family did not complete the journey, but stopped and settled at Haran (Genesis 11:31). In today's story, God called Abraham to complete the journey.

Today's story took place before God changed Abraham's name from Abram to Abraham and his wife's name from Sarai to Sarah. To avoid confusion for children, the names Abraham and Sarah are used here.

God's call required a lot of trust on Abraham's part. God asked Abraham to leave his country, his extended family, and his home. Abraham's wife Sarah traveled with him, as did Lot, Abraham's nephew who was under Abraham's care. In return for Abraham's trust and obedience, God made some promises: God would (1) make Abraham a great nation, (2) bless Abraham, (3) make Abraham's name great, and (4) bless those who bless Abraham (and curse those who curse him). Abraham obeyed God, setting in motion events that would continue long after Abraham's life was over.

You may recall that, during the Creation story, God blessed the animals and humans after they were created. Blessing is a key theme throughout Genesis. A blessing is an approval or affirmation. Blessings may come directly from God, as in this story, or be mediated through people.

Devotion

Think about your spiritual ancestry. Who are the people who came before you and influenced your faith? It might be a person from history, like Martin Luther or John Wesley, or it might be someone in your family, like a grandmother or a grandfather. It even might be someone outside your family, like a teacher or a coach. Take a few moments to thank God for all the people on your spiritual family tree. Remember that, as a teacher, you are now part of the ancestry of the children you teach. Thank you for answering the call to this important task.

biblestorybasics.com

BASIC _____

Plan

Bible Beginnings
Welcome
Picture the Bible Story
Bible Puzzle
Bible Play

Into the Bible
Time for the Bible Story
Open the Bible
Experience the Bible Story
Say the Bible Verse

Bible Connections
Camel Capers
Make a Desert Picture

Live the Bible
Fizzy Stars
I Am One of Them

Express Praise
Praise and Pray
Blessing

Bible Beginnings

Welcome

Supplies: Class Pack—Attendance Chart, p. 2; CD-ROM; CD player; tape; offering basket

- Display the attendance chart (Class Pack) and "Unit 2 Bible Verse Picture" (Class Pack—p. 2) at the children's eye level.

- Play "The B-I-B-L-E" from the CD-ROM (lyrics on p. 86) as you welcome each child.

- Have each child mark his or her attendance.

- Show the children where to place their offerings on the worship table.

SAY: Our Bible story is about a man named Abraham and his wife Sarah. God talked to Abraham and told him to move his whole family to a new land. Abraham and his family did what God wanted them to do.

- Point out the Bible verse picture, and say the Bible verse for the children.

Picture the Bible Story

Supplies: Leader Guide—p. 42, crayons or markers, star stickers

- Photocopy "Abraham Looks at the Stars" for each child.

- Give each child the picture.

SAY: God told Abraham that Abraham would have as many children as the number of stars in the sky.

- Encourage the children to decorate the picture with crayons or markers.

- Let the children add star stickers in the sky.

Bible Puzzle

Supplies: Bible Story Leaflets—Session 6, p. 4; crayons or markers

- Give each child a copy of today's Bible Story Leaflet.

- Encourage the children to find five things in the picture on the bottom that are different from the picture on the top.

SAY: God talked to Abraham and told him to move his whole family to a new land. Abraham and his family did what God wanted them to do.

Bible Play

Supplies: small tent or sheet

- Encourage the children to help you set up the tent. If you are using a sheet, drape the sheet over a table.

SAY: God told Abraham to move his whole family to a new land. While Abraham and Sarah were moving, they lived in a tent.

- Have the children help you take down the tent. Move the tent to a different place in the room, and then set up the tent again.

Into the Bible

Time for the Bible Story

SAY: Let's pretend that we are moving with Abraham and Sarah to our Story Area.

• Sing the following song to the tune of "Are You Sleeping?" ("Frère Jacques") as the children move. End the song in your large group area.

SING: God called Abraham, God called Abraham.
  "Go this way. Go this way.
  "To a land I show you. To a land a show you.
  "Go today. Go today."

• Have the children sit down.

SAY: Our Bible story is about a man named Abraham and his wife Sarah. God talked to Abraham and told him to move his whole family to a new land.

Open the Bible

Supplies: Bible Basics Storybook—pp. 22-23

• Tell the children the story "Abraham and Sarah."

Experience the Bible Story

Supplies: CEB Bible; Bible Story Leaflets—Session 6, pp. 2-3

• Show the children the Bible.

TODAY'S BIBLE TOOL: The books of the Bible have many chapters.

SAY: Today, our Bible story is from the Old Testament. It is in a book named Genesis. Genesis is divided into many chapters. The first chapter tells the story of Creation.

• Show children the first chapter of Genesis.

SAY: Today, our story starts in the twelfth chapter of Genesis. Let's count to 12.

• Count to 12 as you turn the pages in your Bible.

SAY: Listen and watch as I tell the story. You can help me do some motions.

• Place the leaflet inside the Bible. Tell the children the story "Abraham and Sarah" from the leaflet, and encourage them to do the suggested motions with you.

ASK: How do you think Abraham and Sarah felt as they moved to a new place?

Say the Bible Verse

Supplies: Class Pack—p. 2, Leader Guide—p. 89

• Show the children the Bible verse picture (Class Pack). Repeat the verse.

• Teach the children signs in American Sign Language to go along with the verse (Leader Guide).

• Encourage the children to make the signs as they say the verse again.

Bible Connections

Camel Capers

Supplies: two plastic shopping bags, clothing or towels

• Pack the two bags with clothing or towels. Tie the handles of the two bags together.

SAY: Our Bible story is about Abraham and Sarah. God talked to Abraham and told him to move his whole family to a new land. Let's pretend to be camels traveling with Abraham and Sarah. I'll pack Abraham and Sarah's things on your back.

• Have the children line up on one side of the room. Choose a child to begin.

• Have the child bend over. Place the bags across the child's back like saddlebags. Encourage the child to walk like a camel to the other side of the room and back again.

• Remove the bags, and place them over the next child's back. Continue until every child has had an opportunity to be a camel.

Make a Desert Picture

Supplies: construction paper, scissors, shallow trays or box lids, colored craft sand

• Cut a piece of construction paper in half. Then cut each half in half again. Fold the fourth in half to make a tent. You will need one tent for each child. The paper tents will represent Abraham and Sarah's tent.

SAY: Let's make a desert picture to help us remember the story of Abraham and Sarah. First, we will add sand.

• Give each child a piece of construction paper.

• Have each child use the glue to make designs on his or her paper.

• Place each child's paper into a shallow tray or box lid. Let the children sprinkle sand over their papers. Have the children shake off the excess sand into a trash container.

• Give each child a paper tent.

SAY: God talked to Abraham and told him to move his whole family to a new land. Abraham and Sarah packed up their tent and all their things and went where God told them to go.

• Encourage the children to move their tent to different places on their paper.

Live the Bible

Fizzy Stars

Supplies: tray or shallow pan, star cookie cutters, spoons, baking soda, vinegar, eye droppers

• Place a tray or shallow pan on the table. Place star cookie cutters in the pan.

• Spoon baking soda inside the cookie cutters.

- Help each child fill an eye dropper with vinegar and squirt the vinegar onto the baking soda inside one of the star cookie cutters. Watch the star fizz.

TIP: You may help each child spoon or pour the vinegar onto the baking soda if you don't have eye droppers.

SAY: God told Abraham that Abraham would have as many children as the number of stars in the sky. God meant that Abraham would have lots of children and grandchildren and great-grandchildren—too many to count. God said, "Look up at the sky and count the stars... This is how many children you will have" (Genesis 15:5). This is our Bible verse.

- Have the children repeat the Bible verse after you.

SAY: Abraham and Sarah's family became God's people. We're all God's people.

I Am One of Them

Supplies: paper plates; crayons or markers; red, yellow, brown, and black yarn; scissors; glue

SAY: Abraham and Sarah's family became God's people. We're all God's people.

- Give each child a paper plate. Encourage each child to use crayons or markers to add eyes, a nose, and a mouth to the paper plate.

- Cut yarn into short pieces. Let the children glue the yarn pieces on their paper plates to make hair.

- Sing the song "Father Abraham" while the children hold their paper plates in front of their faces. (If you don't know the lyrics to the song, you can find them on the Internet.)

TIP: Change the words "Father Abraham had many sons" to "Father Abraham had many children."

Express Praise

Praise and Pray

Supplies: CD-ROM, CD player

- Sing with the children the song "Hear Us As We Pray" from the CD-ROM (lyrics on p. 87). Encourage the children to name any prayer requests.

PRAY: Thank you, God, for stories about Abraham and Sarah. We know that we are your people. Amen.

Blessing

Supplies: none

- Go to a child. Use a finger to draw a star on the back of the child's hand.

SAY: *(Child's name)*, you are part of God's family.

- Continue until you have blessed each child.

Abraham Looks at the Stars

Look up at the sky and count the stars...
This is how many children you will have. (Genesis 15:5)

Permission is granted to duplicate this page for local church use only. © 2019 Abingdon Press.

Abraham and Lot

Bible Verse: Look up at the sky and count the stars... This is how many children you will have. (Genesis 15:5)

Bible Story: Genesis 13:1-12

Bible Background

Last week, we heard about God telling Abraham to move. It's after this move that we encounter Abraham in our story this week. In response to God's instruction, Abraham left the city of Haran, taking with him his wife Sarah and his nephew Lot. Their lifestyle was a nomadic one, traveling with their flocks and herds. They moved around the area, making and breaking camp as needed to find food for their animals.

Abraham's and Lot's flocks had grown so large that it was becoming increasingly difficult for them to share the same land. Their shepherds began to quarrel. Historically, it was not uncommon for nomads to quarrel over pastures and water sources for their animals. It was also common for families to separate and spread out when it became necessary. Thus, Abraham and Lot's eventual separation is not a reason to think poorly of them for not being able to get along. Separation was a responsible way of addressing crowded conditions.

Of course, the separation did not have to occur peacefully. But because Abraham trusted God and valued familial peace, he offered Lot first choice of land. When we trust God's promises and remember God's blessings, it is easier to be generous.

Help the children understand that they can solve their problems in peaceful ways. Even young children struggle and fight. As a teacher, you can help children find peaceful solutions to their problems.

Devotion

Why do families fight? Sometimes families have differing opinions. God reminds us that we can be different and still respect and love one another. God makes us unique but always wants us to be loving, even when we disagree or fight. Is there conflict in your family right now? What is the best way you can respond to the conflict? How can you show God's love to everyone in your family? Pray, "God, thank you for Abraham's example. Teach us to trust you more. Show us how to resolve conflict in the best way. Amen."

biblestorybasics.com

BASIC

Plan

Bible Beginnings
Welcome
Picture the Bible Story
Bible Puzzle
Bible Play

Into the Bible
Time for the Bible Story
Open the Bible
Experience the Bible Story
Say the Bible Verse

Bible Connections
Meadow Murals
Handprint Sheep

Live the Bible
Play a Memory Game
Share

Express Praise
Praise and Pray
Blessing

Bible Beginnings

Welcome

Supplies: Class Pack—Attendance Chart, p. 2; CD-ROM; CD player; tape; offering basket

- Display the attendance chart (Class Pack) and "Unit 2 Bible Verse Picture" (Class Pack—p. 2) at the children's eye level.

- Play "The B-I-B-L-E" from the CD-ROM (lyrics on p. 86) as you welcome each child.

- Have each child mark his or her attendance.

- Show the children where to place their offerings on the worship table.

SAY: Our Bible story is about Abraham and his nephew Lot. When God told Abraham to move to a new land, Lot moved with him. Abraham and Lot chose to share.

- Point out the Bible verse picture, and say the Bible verse for the children.

Picture the Bible Story

Supplies: Leader Guide—p. 48, crayons or markers, scissors, resealable plastic bags

- Photocopy "Abraham and Lot" for each child.

- Give each child the picture.

SAY: This is a picture of Abraham and his nephew Lot. When God told Abraham to move to a new land, Lot moved with him.

- Encourage the children to decorate the picture with crayons or markers. Once each child is finished decorating the picture, cut the picture into puzzle pieces. Have the children put their puzzle pieces in a resealable plastic bag to take home.

Bible Puzzle

Supplies: Bible Story Leaflets—Session 7, p. 4; crayons or markers

- Give each child a copy of today's Bible Story Leaflet.

- Encourage the children to use a crayon or marker to follow the path from Abraham to Abraham and the path from Lot to Lot.

SAY: Abraham and Lot had lots of sheep and goats. They had so many sheep and goats that there was not enough grass to feed all the animals. So, Abraham and Lot chose to live in different places.

Bible Play

Supplies: Leader Guide—p. 92; crayons or markers

- Photocopy "Abraham and Sarah's Tent" for each child.

- Give each child the picture.

SAY: God told Abraham to move his family to a new land. While Abraham, Sarah, and Lot were moving, they lived in a tent.

- Encourage the children to decorate the picture with crayons or markers.

Into the Bible

Time for the Bible Story

SAY: Let's pretend that we are moving with Abraham and Sarah to our Story Area.

• Sing the following song to the tune of "Are You Sleeping?" ("Frère Jacques") as the children move. End the song in your large group area.

SING: God called Abraham, God called Abraham.
    "Go this way. Go this way.
    "To a land I show you. To a land a show you.
    "Go today. Go today."

• Have the children sit down.

SAY: Our Bible story is about Abraham and his nephew Lot. Abraham and Lot chose to share.

Open the Bible

Supplies: Bible Basics Storybook—pp. 24-25

• Tell the children the story "Abraham and Lot."

Experience the Bible Story

Supplies: CEB Bible; Bible Story Leaflets—Session 7, pp. 2-3

• Show the children the Bible.

TODAY'S BIBLE TOOL: The books of the Bible have many chapters.

SAY: Today, our Bible story is from the Old Testament. It is in a book named Genesis. Genesis is divided into many chapters. The first chapter tells the story of Creation.

• Show children the first chapter of Genesis.

SAY: Today, our story is from thirteenth chapter of Genesis. Listen and watch as I tell the story. You can help me do some sounds and motions.

• Place the leaflet inside the Bible. Tell the children the story "Abraham and Lot" from the leaflet, and encourage them to do the suggested sounds and motions with you.

ASK: How do you think Abraham and Lot felt when they moved to different places?

Say the Bible Verse

Supplies: Class Pack—p. 2, Leader Guide—p. 89

• Show the children the Bible verse picture (Class Pack). Repeat the verse.

• Teach the children signs in American Sign Language to go along with the verse (Leader Guide).

• Encourage the children to make the signs as they say the verse again.

Bible Connections

Meadow Murals

Supplies: two pieces of green or brown construction paper, tape, cotton balls, glue

• Tape the two pieces of construction paper together to make one long sheet.

SAY: Today, our Bible story is about Abraham and his nephew Lot. Abraham and Lot had many, many sheep and goats. Let's pretend this is the field where Abraham and Lot are keeping their sheep and goats. Let's add lots of sheep to the field.

• Let the children glue cotton balls all over the taped pieces of paper. Encourage the children to glue on lots of cotton balls.

SAY: Oh no! There are too many sheep. There isn't enough grass to feed all of them.

ASK: What should we do?

• Encourage the children to give suggestions.

SAY: I know! I'll take Lot's sheep and move them over here.

• Remove the tape connecting the two pieces of construction paper. Place one of the pieces on one side of the room.

SAY: And I'll move Abraham's sheep over here.

• Place the second piece on the other side of the room.

SAY: Abraham and Lot moved to different places. Abraham let Lot choose the land Lot wanted.

Handprint Sheep

Supplies: black construction paper, crayons or pencils, scissors, cotton balls, glue

SAY: Abraham and Lot had many sheep and goats. Let's make our own sheep.

• Give each child a piece of black construction paper.

• Have each child spread apart the fingers on one hand and place that hand on his or her piece of construction paper. Help each child trace around the hand.

• Cut out each child's handprint.

• Have each child turn the handprint so that the fingers and thumb are facing downward.

• Let each child glue cotton balls on the palm area of his or her handprint.

• Have the children place their sheep in the middle of the floor.

SAY: We have too many sheep!

ASK: What should we do?

• Have the children move the sheep into two different areas of the room.

SAY: Abraham and Lot wanted to live peacefully. They chose to move to different parts of the land so that there would be enough grass for all their sheep and goats.

Live the Bible

Play a Memory Game

Supplies: tray; a box of crayons, two or three markers, scissors, paper, glue, toys, or other things that the children can share; towel or piece of cloth

• Place the items that the children can share on the tray. Show the tray to the children.

SAY: These are all things we can share. Try to remember everything on the tray.

• Cover the tray with a towel or a piece of cloth.

• Have the children close their eyes. Remove one item from under the fabric, and hide it behind your back.

• Uncover the tray, and have the children open their eyes.

• Let the children guess which item is missing.

• Play this game several times.

SAY: Abraham and Lot wanted to live peacefully, so they decided to share the land. These are all things we can share.

Share

Supplies: blocks, art supplies, toys

• Let the children play with blocks, art supplies, and toys.

• Encourage the children to share as they play.

SAY: Our room has many things that we can share.

Express Praise

Praise and Pray

Supplies: CD-ROM, CD player

• Sing with the children the song "Hear Us As We Pray" from the CD-ROM (lyrics on p. 87). Encourage the children to name any prayer requests.

PRAY: Thank you, God, for teaching us how to share. Amen.

Blessing

Supplies: none

• Go to a child. Use a finger to draw a star on the back of the child's hand.

SAY: *(Child's name)*, you are part of God's family.

• Continue until you have blessed each child.

Abraham and Lot

Look up at the sky and count the stars...
This is how many children you will have. (Genesis 15:5)

Permission is granted to duplicate this page for local church use only. © 2019 Abingdon Press.

The Birth of Isaac

Bible Verse: Look up at the sky and count the stars... This is how many children you will have. (Genesis 15:5)

Bible Story: Genesis 18:1-15; 21:1-7

Bible Background

When Abraham was 99 years old, God appeared to Abraham again. Unlike previous encounters, Abraham was not aware God was visiting him. To Abraham's knowledge, he merely entertained three men who appeared near his tent. Abraham extended hospitality to the men—he ran to greet them, invited them to stay, provided water to wash their feet, and served them a feast. To us, this may seem like an unusual response to strangers appearing at one's home, but hospitality to strangers was important in ancient times. There was a protocol to be followed. Custom required that the owner of a house take care of any stranger he invited to stay. Once a host extended hospitality to a traveler, he was expected to treat him as one of the family.

During their visit, the men told Abraham that he and his wife would have a son in a year's time. Sarah, who was listening at the door of the tent, laughed to herself. In an earlier encounter with God (Genesis 17:17), Abraham had laughed in response to this same pronouncement. After all, Sarah was well past childbearing age by this time. As much as Abraham and Sarah trusted God, they were finding it difficult to trust this particular promise.

But God did fulfill the promise, and Sarah gave birth to a son. Abraham and Sarah named him Isaac, which means "He laughs."

Abraham did have many descendants. Christians and Jews trace their ancestry back to Abraham through his son Isaac. Muslims also trace their ancestry back to Abraham through Ishmael, Abraham's son with Hagar.

Devotion

God had made a promise to Abraham and Sarah, but years and years had gone by. They still had no children. Read Genesis 16:1-16 for the story of what happened when Sarah and Abraham decided to take matters into their own hands. Sometimes, like Sarah, we get impatient and want God's plan to happen right now. What are you waiting for? Remember, God is with you.

biblestorybasics.com

BASIC

Plan

Bible Beginnings
Welcome
Picture the Bible Story
Bible Puzzle
Bible Play

Into the Bible
Time for the Bible Story
Open the Bible
Experience the Bible Story
Say the Bible Verse

Bible Connections
Wash Babies
The Story of Isaac

Live the Bible
Name Cards
Laughter Exercises

Express Praise
Praise and Pray
Blessing

Bible Beginnings

Welcome

Supplies: Class Pack—Attendance Chart, p. 2; CD-ROM; CD player; tape; offering basket

- Display the attendance chart (Class Pack) and "Unit 2 Bible Verse Picture" (Class Pack—p. 2) at the children's eye level.

- Play "The B-I-B-L-E" from the CD-ROM (lyrics on p. 86) as you welcome each child.

- Have each child mark his or her attendance.

- Show the children where to place their offerings on the worship table.

SAY: Our Bible story is about waiting. God promised Abraham that he would have many children. But many years had gone by, and Abraham and Sarah still did not have any children. Abraham and Sarah were very old. Abraham was 99 years old!

- Point out the Bible verse picture, and say the Bible verse for the children.

Picture the Bible Story

Supplies: Leader Guide—p. 54, crayons or markers

- Photocopy "Family Portrait" for each child.

- Give each child the picture.

SAY: This is a picture of Abraham and Sarah with their new baby. God kept the promise. Sarah and Abraham had a baby and named him Isaac.

- Encourage the children to decorate the picture with crayons or markers.

Bible Puzzle

Supplies: Bible Story Leaflets—Session 8, p. 4; crayons or markers

- Give each child a copy of today's Bible Story Leaflet.

- Encourage the children to circle the Bible-times items Sarah and Abraham can use to take care of baby Isaac.

SAY: God kept the promise. Sarah and Abraham had a baby and named him Isaac.

ASK: How do you think Sarah and Abraham felt when they had baby Isaac?

Bible Play

Supplies: small tent or sheet, baby doll, doll blanket

- Encourage the children to help you set up the tent. If you are using a sheet, drape the sheet over a table.

- Add a baby doll and doll blanket to your tent area. Encourage the children to take care of the baby.

ASK: What do you think Sarah and Abraham did to take care of their baby?

Into the Bible

Time for the Bible Story

SAY: Let's pretend that we are moving with Abraham, Sarah, and baby Isaac to the Story Area.

• Sing the following song to the tune of "Are You Sleeping?" ("Frère Jacques") as the children move. End the song in your large group area.

SING: God called Abraham, God called Abraham.
"Go this way. Go this way.
"To a land I show you. To a land a show you.
"Go today. Go today."

• Have the children sit down.

SAY: Our Bible story is about Abraham, Sarah, and Isaac. Isaac was the baby God promised Abraham and Sarah.

Open the Bible

Supplies: Bible Basics Storybook—pp. 26-27

• Tell the children the story "The Birth of Isaac."

Experience the Bible Story

Supplies: CEB Bible; Bible Story Leaflets—Session 8, pp. 2-3

• Show the children the Bible.

TODAY'S BIBLE TOOL: The books of the Bible have many chapters.

SAY: Today, our Bible story is from the Old Testament. It is in a book named Genesis. Genesis is divided into many chapters. The first chapter tells the story of Creation.

• Show children the first chapter of Genesis.

SAY: Today, our story is from two chapters in Genesis—chapters 18 and 21.

• Show the children Genesis 18 and Genesis 21.

SAY: Listen and watch as I tell the story. You can help me by pretending to laugh.

• Place the leaflet inside the Bible. Tell the children the story "The Birth of Isaac" from the leaflet, and encourage them to pretend to laugh when suggested.

ASK: How do you think Sarah and Abraham felt when they had baby Isaac?

Say the Bible Verse

Supplies: Class Pack—p. 2, Leader Guide—p. 89

• Show the children the Bible verse picture (Class Pack). Repeat the verse.

• Teach the children signs in American Sign Language to go along with the verse (Leader Guide).

• Encourage the children to make the signs as they say the verse again.

Bible Connections

Wash Babies

Supplies: plastic tub, water, waterproof baby dolls, towels

• Partially fill the plastic tub with water.

• Let the children give baths to the baby dolls.

SAY: Today, our Bible story is about Abraham and Sarah. God promised Abraham and Sarah that they would have many children. But many years had gone by, and Abraham and Sarah still did not have any children. Abraham and Sarah were very old. Abraham was 99 years old!

ASK: Do you think that Sarah and Abraham were too old to have a baby?

SAY: Sarah thought she was too old, but God kept the promise. Sarah and Abraham had a baby and named him Isaac.

The Story of Isaac

Supplies: none

• Have the children move to an open area of the room.

• Say the following action poem, and lead the children in doing the motions.

Abraham and Sarah were growing old.
(Hunch your back; walk in place.)
Oh, how they prayed for a baby to hold.
(Fold your hands.)
God said to each of them, "It shall be done."
(Cross your hands over your heart.)

Soon they were blessed with a beautiful son.
(Pretend to rock a baby.)
They named him Isaac, and he brought them much joy.
(Smile.)
He grew and he grew to be a strong boy.
(Crouch down, then gradually stand up.)

SAY: God kept the promise. Sarah and Abraham had a baby and named him Isaac. Isaac grew up and had children. Then his children grew up and had children. Then their children grew up and had even more children. Abraham's family kept growing and growing. Abraham's family became the people of God. We're part of God's family. We're people of God.

Live the Bible

Name Cards

Supplies: construction paper, scissors, permanent marker, stickers, crayons or markers

• Cut several sheets of construction paper in half.

• Use a permanent marker to write each child's name in large block letters on a separate half sheet of construction paper.

• Give each child his or her name card.

SAY: Sarah and Abraham were so happy when their baby was born that they laughed for joy. They named him Isaac, which means "He laughs." Your parents gave you your own special name.

• Encourage the children to decorate their card with stickers and crayons or markers.

• Have the children hold their name card and move to one side of the room. Stand on the opposite side of the room.

SAY: (Child's name), God promised to be with you. Jump toward me three times.

• Continue calling each child's name and telling him or her how many jumps to move. Play the game until all the children have crossed the room.

Laughter Exercises

Supplies: none

SAY: Sarah laughed when she heard the visitors tell Abraham she would have a baby.

ASK: Why do you think she laughed? What did Abraham and Sarah name their baby? What does the name *Isaac* mean? *(He laughs.)*

SAY: Laughter is good for our bodies. It makes us feel better. Let's try some laughter exercises.

• Have the children stand in a circle. Encourage the children to place their hands on their stomach and shout, "Ha, ha, ha! Ho, ho, ho! Yeah!"

• Have the children repeat the shout. This time, have them clap their hands as they shout, "Ha, ha, ha! Ho, ho, ho!" Have them raise a fist in the air as they shout, "Yeah!"

• Have the children repeat the shout again. This time, have them clap their hands and stomp their feet as they shout, "Ha, ha, ha! Ho, ho, ho!" Have them raise both fists in the air as they shout, "Yeah!"

ASK: How do you feel?

Express Praise

Praise and Pray

Supplies: CD-ROM, CD player

• Sing with the children the song "Hear Us As We Pray" from the CD-ROM (lyrics on p. 87). Encourage the children to name any prayer requests.

PRAY: Thank you, God, for teaching us how to laugh. Amen.

Blessing

Supplies: none

• Go to a child. Use a finger to draw a star on the back of the child's hand.

SAY: (Child's name), you are part of God's family.

• Continue until you have blessed each child.

Family Portrait

Look up at the sky and count the stars...
This is how many children you will have. (Genesis 15:5)

Permission is granted to duplicate this page for local church use only. © 2019 Abingdon Press.

Isaac and Rebekah

Bible Verse: Look up at the sky and count the stars… This is how many children you will have. (Genesis 15:5)

Bible Story: Genesis 24:1-67

biblestorybasics.com

Bible Background

Last week, we read of Isaac's birth, but now we will fast-forward through the years to today's story. By this time, Isaac was grown and ready to marry. Abraham, who was already 100 years old when Isaac was born, had not gotten any younger. Abraham called his servant and made him promise not to let Isaac marry a Canaanite woman. Remember that Abraham had moved to Canaan following God's instructions. Abraham, who had been faithful to God, did not want his son to marry a woman who did not worship God.

Abraham decided to send his servant back to Haran, where Abraham had been living before God told him to move, to find a wife among Abraham's family still living there. We may wonder, as Abraham's servant did, why Abraham didn't send Isaac to find his own wife. But if Isaac had gone to Haran himself, he might have decided to settle there with his wife's family. Since God called Abraham from Haran to Canaan, this would have been going backward in God's plan for Abraham's family.

The servant Abraham sent to find a wife for Isaac asked God to guide the process. God was not only with Abraham; God was also with Abraham's family and servants.

Rebekah showed up at the well while the servant was praying to God for help. The servant saw traits in Rebekah that would make her a good wife for Isaac. Rebekah was kind to the servant without knowing who he was. Rebekah offered a drink to him and his camels, which was a monumental task for a young woman. When the servant became aware of Rebekah's kindness, he knew God had heard and answered his prayer. Rebekah was God's choice for Isaac's wife.

Devotion

Abraham's faith influenced not only his family, but also those in his household. It is evident to believers that the blessings of faith extend far beyond ourselves. How does your belief in God show up in your daily life? How does your faith influence your child? others in your family? others outside your family? Pray, "God, help us be so faithful that others will be influenced by how we live out our faith. Amen."

Plan

Bible Beginnings
Welcome
Picture the Bible Story
Bible Puzzle
Bible Play

Into the Bible
Time for the Bible Story
Open the Bible
Experience the Bible Story
Say the Bible Verse

Bible Connections
Water at the Well
Camel Relay

Live the Bible
Prayer Bracelets
If We Can Pray When…

Express Praise
Praise and Pray
Blessing

Bible Beginnings

Welcome

Supplies: Class Pack—Attendance Chart, p. 2; CD-ROM; CD player; tape; offering basket

• Display the attendance chart (Class Pack) and "Unit 2 Bible Verse Picture" (Class Pack—p. 2) at the children's eye level.

• Play "The B-I-B-L-E" from the CD-ROM (lyrics on p. 86) as you welcome each child.

• Have each child mark his or her attendance.

• Show the children where to place their offerings on the worship table.

SAY: Isaac grew from a baby to a man. Grown-up Isaac married a woman named Rebekah.

• Point out the Bible verse picture, and say the Bible verse for the children.

Picture the Bible Story

Supplies: Leader Guide—p. 60, crayons or markers

• Photocopy "Rebekah Watering the Camels" for each child.

• Give each child the picture.

SAY: This is a picture of a woman named Rebekah watering camels with water she got from a well. Getting water to drink is an important part of today's Bible story. In Bible times, people got water from a well. They collected water in clay jars to carry home. Sometimes a women would carry a water jar on her head.

• Encourage the children to decorate the picture with crayons or markers.

Bible Puzzle

Supplies: Bible Story Leaflets—Session 9, p. 4; crayons or markers

• Give each child a copy of today's Bible Story Leaflet.

• Encourage the children to use a crayon or marker to trace the path from the servant to Rebekah.

SAY: Abraham sent a servant to find a wife for Isaac. The servant prayed for God to help him find the right wife. When the servant met Rebekah, he knew she was the woman God had chosen to be Isaac's wife.

Bible Play

Supplies: small tent or sheet, Bible-times costumes

• Encourage the children to help you set up the tent. If you are using a sheet, drape the sheet over a table.

• Encourage the children to dress up in Bible-times costumes and pretend to live in the tent.

ASK: What are some things you would do if you lived in a tent?

Into the Bible

Time for the Bible Story

SAY: Let's pretend that we are traveling with the servant to our Story Area.

• Sing the following song to the tune of "Are You Sleeping?" ("Frère Jacques") as the children move. End the song in your large group area.

SING: God called Abraham, God called Abraham.
"Go this way. Go this way.
"To a land I show you. To a land a show you.
"Go today. Go today."

• Have the children sit down.

SAY: God was with Abraham and Sarah as they traveled to a new land. God was with the servant when he traveled to find Isaac's wife. God is with us wherever we go.

Open the Bible

Supplies: Bible Basics Storybook—pp. 28-29

• Tell the children the story "Isaac and Rebekah."

Experience the Bible Story

Supplies: CEB Bible; Bible Story Leaflets—Session 9, pp. 2-3

• Show the children the Bible.

TODAY'S BIBLE TOOL: The books of the Bible have many chapters.

SAY: Our Bible story today is from the Old Testament. It is in a book named Genesis. Genesis is divided into many chapters. The first chapter tells the story of Creation.

• Show the children the first chapter of Genesis.

SAY: Today, our story is from chapter 24.

• Show the children Genesis 24.

SAY: Listen and watch as I tell the story. You can help me do some motions.

• Place the leaflet inside the Bible. Tell the children the story "Isaac and Rebekah" from the leaflet, and encourage them to do the suggested motions.

ASK: How do you think the servant felt when Abraham asked the servant to find a wife for Isaac? How do you think Isaac and Rebekah felt when they married?

Say the Bible Verse

Supplies: Class Pack—p. 2, Leader Guide—p. 89

• Show the children the Bible verse picture (Class Pack). Repeat the verse.

• Teach the children signs in American Sign Language to go along with the verse (Leader Guide).

• Encourage the children to make the signs as they say the verse again.

Bible Connections

Water at the Well

Supplies: plastic table covering, plastic tub, water, plastic cups, towels

• Cover the table or floor with the covering. Partially fill a plastic tub with water, and place it on top of the covering.

SAY: In Bible times, people got water from wells. A well is a hole in the ground that ends at some kind of underground water. The water is clean and fresh.

• Give each child a plastic cup. Let each child dip his or her plastic cup into the tub to retrieve water and then pour the water back into the well.

SAY: In our Bible story today, Abraham's servant was resting at a well. He prayed for God to help him find the right wife for Isaac. He saw Rebekah getting water from the well. Rebekah offered him water for himself and his ten camels. The servant knew that this kind woman was the wife God had chosen for Isaac.

Camel Relay

Supplies: pitcher, water, paper cups, trash can, towel

• Fill a pitcher with water. Place paper cups and a trash can on one side of the room.

• Pour a small amount of water into each cup.

TIP: Have a towel nearby for spills.

• Split the children into two teams, and have the two teams line up single file on the other side of the room.

SAY: Rebekah was kind enough to give water to the servant's camels. That was a big job because camels can drink a lot of water. One camel can drink over 50 gallons of water in three minutes. Let's pretend to be camels. Go, camels, go!

• Have the first child in line for each team move like a camel to a cup of water. Have the child stop, pick up the cup, drink the water, throw the empty cup into the trash can, and then run back to his or her team.

• Once a child has returned to his or her team, have the next child in line for that team move like a camel to another cup of water. Continue the relay until each child has had a chance to participate.

Live the Bible

Prayer Bracelets

Supplies: construction paper, ruler, scissors, tape, crayons or markers

• Cut construction paper into two-by-eight-inch strips. Each child will need one strip.

SAY: Abraham's servant asked God for help finding a wife for Isaac. We can ask God to help us. When we ask God for help, it is called praying.

• Give each child a strip of construction paper.

ASK: What's something you'd like God to help you with? Do you need help learning how to read? Do you need help remembering to take out the trash? Do you need help remembering to use kind words?

- Have each child write on the strip of paper one word that represents something he or she needs help with. Write the word for younger children.
- Encourage each child to decorate around the word with crayons or markers.
- Place the strip around the child's wrist, and tape the ends together.

SAY: You've made a prayer bracelet. The bracelet can help you remember to ask God for help.

If We Can Pray When...

Supplies: none

- Have the children move to an open area of the room.

SAY: Abraham's servant prayed to God when he needed help finding a wife for Isaac. Let's think about when we can pray. I'm going to suggest some different times when we might be able to pray. If you think what I say is a time when we can pray, I want you to do what I tell you to do.

> **If we can pray when we need help tying our shoes, touch your toes.**
> **If we can pray when we go to bed, yawn and stretch your arms.**
> **If we can pray when we need help learning to throw a ball, jump three times.**
> **If we can pray when we are feeling really sad, turn around two times.**
> **If we can pray before we eat dinner, rub your tummy.**
> **If we can pray with our family and friends, hop on one foot.**

SAY: We can pray to God anytime, anywhere, and about anything. Thank you, God, for hearing us when we pray. Amen.

Express Praise

Praise and Pray

Supplies: CD-ROM, CD player

- Sing with the children the song "Hear Us As We Pray" from the CD-ROM (lyrics on p. 87). Encourage the children to name any prayer requests.

PRAY: Thank you, God, for listening to us when we pray. Amen.

Blessing

Supplies: none

- Go to a child. Use a finger to draw a star on the back of the child's hand.

SAY: *(Child's name)*, you are part of God's family.

- Continue until you have blessed each child.

Rebekah Watering the Camels

Look up at the sky and count the stars...
This is how many children you will have. (Genesis 15:5)

Permission is granted to duplicate this page for local church use only. © 2019 Abingdon Press.

Jacob and Esau

Bible Verse: Every family of earth will be blessed because of you and your descendants. (Genesis 28:14)

Bible Story: Genesis 25:19-28

biblestorybasics.com

Bible Background

Last week, we heard about Isaac and Rebekah. By the time of this week's Bible story, Isaac was a 60-year-old man. Isaac and Rebekah had been married for 20 years, but they did not yet have any children. Isaac prayed and asked God for children, and Rebekah became pregnant with twins.

Rebekah's babies fought with each other before they were born, setting the stage for a complex relationship that lasted throughout their lives. When Rebekah asked God why her pregnancy was so difficult, God told her that two nations were struggling inside of her. Rebekah eventually gave birth to twin boys. Esau was born first, and the second son, Jacob, came out gripping Esau's heel.

Esau and Jacob were fraternal twins. They chose different ways of life, ways that were often in tension. Esau was red and hairy. Esau's name sounds like the Hebrew word *seir*, which means "hairy." Esau was a hunter. He was at home in the wild, on the move with the animals. Jacob was quiet. He chose a more settled, pastoral way of life. Jacob's name may have been derived from the Hebrew word `*aqeb*, which means "heel." Favoritism shown by the parents also added to the tension in the family. Isaac favored Esau, while Jacob was Rebekah's favorite.

This week, we begin a monthlong look at blessings and birthrights. As you teach about blessings and birthrights this month, take the opportunity to let the children know they are blessed. Be sure to participate in the blessing ritual at the end of each session.

Devotion

Even though Jacob and Esau were twins, they were unique. They looked different, but they also liked different things and had different skills. Think about your unique qualities. What do you like about yourself? What things do you like to do? Does the rest of your family like the same things, or do they enjoy different things? Take a few moments to thank God for your unique qualities. You are made in the image of God, and God loves you just as you are. Be yourself!

BASIC

Plan

Bible Beginnings
Welcome
Picture the Bible Story
Bible Puzzle
Bible Play

Into the Bible
Time for the Bible Story
Open the Bible
Experience the Bible Story
Say the Bible Verse

Bible Connections
Twin Relay
Footprint Art

Live the Bible
Alike and Different
Look in the Mirror

Express Praise
Praise and Pray
Blessing

Bible Beginnings

Welcome

Supplies: Class Pack—Attendance Chart, p. 3; CD-ROM; CD player; tape; offering basket

• Display the attendance chart (Class Pack) and "Unit 3 Bible Verse Picture" (Class Pack—p. 3) at the children's eye level.

• Play "The B-I-B-L-E" from the CD-ROM (lyrics on p. 86) as you welcome each child.

• Have each child mark his or her attendance.

• Show the children where to place their offerings on the worship table.

SAY: Isaac and Rebekah had two babies named Jacob and Esau. The babies were twins.

• Point out the Bible verse picture, and say the Bible verse for the children.

Picture the Bible Story

Supplies: Leader Guide—p. 66, crayons or markers

• Photocopy "Jacob and Esau" for each child.

• Give each child the picture.

SAY: Today, our Bible story is about two babies named Jacob and Esau. The babies were twins. Jacob and Esau were born at the same time, but they were not just alike.

• Encourage the children to decorate the picture with crayons or markers.

Bible Puzzle

Supplies: Bible Story Leaflets—Session 10, p. 4; crayons or markers

• Give each child a copy of today's Bible Story Leaflet.

• Encourage the children to find the identical twins.

SAY: Today, our Bible story is about two babies named Jacob and Esau. The babies were twins.

Bible Play

Supplies: baby dolls, baby doll accessories

• Encourage the children to play with the baby dolls and baby doll accessories.

SAY: Isaac and Rebekah had two sons named Jacob and Esau. Jacob and Esau were twins, but they were not just alike. Esau was born first. He had red skin and was hairy. Jacob was born second. His skin was very smooth.

ASK: Do any of these baby dolls look like they could be twins?

SAY: Remember, twins don't have to look exactly alike.

Into the Bible

Time for the Bible Story

SAY: Let's pretend that we are visiting Isaac and Rebekah in our Story Area. We want to see their twin babies.

• Sing the following song to the tune of "She'll Be Coming 'Round the Mountain" as the children move. End the song in your large group area.

SING: Oh, Isaac and Rebekah had two sons.
Oh, Isaac and Rebekah had two sons.
Oh, the first son was named Esau, and the second was named Jacob.
Oh, Isaac and Rebekah had two sons.

• Have the children sit down.

SAY: Today, our Bible story is about Isaac and Rebekah's twins, Jacob and Esau.

Open the Bible

Supplies: Bible Basics Storybook—pp. 30-31

• Tell the children the story "Jacob and Esau."

Experience the Bible Story

Supplies: CEB Bible; Bible Story Leaflets—Session 10, pp. 2-3

• Show the children the Bible.

TODAY'S BIBLE TOOL: The books of the Bible have many chapters.

SAY: Today, our Bible story is from the Old Testament. It is in a book named Genesis. Genesis is divided into many chapters. The first chapter tells the story of Creation.

• Show the children the first chapter of Genesis.

SAY: Today, our story is from chapter 25.

• Show the children Genesis 25.

SAY: Listen and watch as I tell the story. You can help me do sounds and motions.

• Place the leaflet inside the Bible. Tell the children the story "Jacob and Esau" from the leaflet, and encourage them to say the words printed in bold and do the suggested motions with you.

ASK: What were some of the differences between Jacob and Esau?

Say the Bible Verse

Supplies: Class Pack—p. 3, Leader Guide—p. 90

• Show the children the Bible verse picture (Class Pack). Repeat the verse.

• Teach the children signs in American Sign Language to go along with the verse (Leader Guide).

• Encourage the children to make the signs as they say the verse again.

Bible Connections

Twin Relay

Supplies: two baby dolls per team

• Divide the children into teams. Have the teams line up single file on one side of the room.

SAY: Today, our Bible story is about twin brothers named Jacob and Esau. The twins' mother, Rebekah, probably carried both her babies at the same time. Let's pretend to carry Jacob and Esau.

• Give two baby dolls to the first child in line on each team. Have these children carry the baby dolls across the room and then back to their team.

• If a child drops a doll, have the child stop, pick it up, and then continue the relay.

• Once a child has returned to his or her team, have the child give the two baby dolls to the next child in line. Continue until every child has had a turn.

• Encourage the children to cheer for one another.

TIP: Don't make a big deal about one team winning.

Footprint Art

Supplies: nonpermanent ink pads or paper towels, shallow trays, washable paint, spoons; plain paper or construction paper; washable baby dolls; wet wipes

• Provide nonpermanent ink pads, or make paint pads. To make a paint pad, fold several paper towels and place them in the bottom of a shallow tray. Pour washable paint onto the paper towels. Spread the paint over the paper towels with a spoon.

SAY: When babies are born, the hospital makes a footprint. Each baby's footprint is different, just like his or her fingerprints. Let's make footprints for our baby dolls.

• Give each child a piece of paper.

• Let each child press a doll's foot onto an ink pad or a paint pad and then onto the paper to make a footprint.

SAY: Even though each one of us is different, we are all part of God's family.

Live the Bible

Alike and Different

Supplies: none

• Have the children sit down in an open area of the room.

• Choose two children to stand together in front of the remaining children.

SAY: Let's look at (names of the two children). Tell me how these two people are alike and how they are different.

• Encourage the children to compare the children in front. Keep comments positive.

- Choose another pair of children to come to the front. Continue the game until every child has been compared with another child.

ASK: Do you think there are any two people who are exactly alike in every way? How were Jacob and Esau different from each other?

Look in the Mirror

Supplies: aluminum foil or reflective mylar sheets; scissors; small paper plates; glue; craft supplies such as rickrack, yarn, large sequins, small pom-poms, and large buttons; stickers; tape; craft sticks

- Cut aluminum foil or reflective mylar sheets into four-inch circles. Each child will need a circle.

SAY: When we look in a mirror we see ourselves. We can see how we are different and how we are the same. Let's make mirrors.

- Give each child a plate and a circle. Have the child glue the circle in the middle of the plate. This will be the reflective part of the mirror.

- Let the children decorate around the mylar circle. They might glue on rickrack, yarn, large sequins, small pom-poms, or large buttons. They might also add stickers.

- Help each child tape a craft stick to the back of his or her decorated mirror to make a handle.

- Encourage the children to look in their mirrors.

SAY: When I look in the mirror, I can see part of God's family—that's me!

Express Praise

Praise and Pray

Supplies: CD-ROM, CD player

- Sing with the children the song "Hear Us As We Pray" from the CD-ROM (lyrics on p. 87). Encourage the children to name any prayer requests.

PRAY: Thank you, God, for making each one of us part of your family. Amen.

Blessing

Supplies: Leader Guide—p. 12 or earth ball

- Have the children sit in a circle.

- Hand the ball to one child. Have that child stand up.

TIP: If you do not have an earth ball, photocopy "God Created the World" and use the picture in place of the ball.

SAY: (Child's name), you are a blessing to every family of earth.

- Have the child give the ball to the next child in the circle. Have that child stand. Bless that child. Continue until you have blessed each child.

Jacob and Esau

Every family of earth will be blessed because of you
and your descendants. (Genesis 28:14)

Permission is granted to duplicate this page for local church use only. © 2019 Abingdon Press.

The Birthright

Bible Verse: Every family of earth will be blessed because of you and your descendants. (Genesis 28:14)

Bible Story: Genesis 25:29-34

biblestorybasics.com

Bible Background

Today, we will hear more about Esau and Jacob, the twin sons of Isaac and Rebekah. As the elder son, Esau was entitled to the birthright. The birthright was a blessing and conferral of rights usually passed on to the eldest son in a family. Israel and some other ancient cultures gave special privileges to the oldest son in a family. The birthright brought with it a leadership role in the family and a larger share of the inheritance. Although the birthright usually was passed on to the eldest son, some stories of the time indicate that it could be forfeited.

In today's story, Esau sold his birthright to Jacob for a bowl of stew. The red color of the stew was linked to the nation of Esau's descendants. The nation was named Edom, which means "red." When Esau requested the "red stuff," the nation of Edom became second to the future nation of Israel, all because Esau sold his birthright for a bowl of stew (Genesis 25:30).

Neither Esau nor Jacob comes off looking particularly good in this story. Jacob was conniving and took advantage of Esau at a weak moment to cheat him out of his birthright. Esau was not very smart, willing to sell the privileges associated with the birthright for a bowl of stew. This is the continuing story of God's people—they are human and imperfect, but they are always loved by God.

Devotion

You may have heard the statement "Let go, and let God." This is great advice, but it is often hard for us to live out. Like Esau, we want things now. Have you ever tried to force things to happen the way you thought they should? Were you happy with the results? Why or why not? Read Psalm 130.

BASIC
Plan

Bible Beginnings
Welcome
Picture the Bible Story
Bible Puzzle
Bible Play

Into the Bible
Time for the Bible Story
Open the Bible
Experience the Bible Story
Say the Bible Verse

Bible Connections
Explain Birthright
Bowl-a-rama

Live the Bible
Ready, Set...
Decorate a Stew Bowl

Express Praise
Praise and Pray
Blessing

Bible Beginnings

Welcome

Supplies: Class Pack—Attendance Chart, p. 3; CD-ROM; CD player; tape; offering basket

- Display the attendance chart (Class Pack) and "Unit 3 Bible Verse Picture" (Class Pack—p. 3) at the children's eye level.
- Play "The B-I-B-L-E" from the CD-ROM (lyrics on p. 86) as you welcome each child.
- Have each child mark his or her attendance.
- Show the children where to place their offerings on the worship table.

SAY: Today, our Bible story is about Jacob and Esau. Jacob and Esau were no longer babies. They had grown up into young men.

- Point out the Bible verse picture, and say the Bible verse for the children.

Picture the Bible Story

Supplies: Leader Guide—p. 72, crayons or markers, tape

- Photocopy "Twins" for each child.
- Give each child the picture.

SAY: This a picture of what Jacob and Esau might have looked like.

ASK: Which boy do you think is Jacob? Which boy do you think is Esau?

- Encourage the children to decorate the picture with crayons or markers.
- Help each child fold the picture so that Jacob is on one side and Esau is on the other. Tape the top and the side of the folded page together, leaving the bottom open.
- Show the children how to put a hand through the bottom of the folded page to use it as a puppet. Save the puppets to use when you tell the Bible story.

Bible Puzzle

Supplies: Bible Story Leaflets—Session 11, p. 4; crayons or markers

- Give each child a copy of today's Bible Story Leaflet.

SAY: In our Bible story today, Jacob made stew. Circle the things you think belong in stew. Cross out the things you think don't belong in stew.

Bible Play

Supplies: paper bowls, spoons, plastic food, unbreakable items that would not go in stew

SAY: A bowl of stew is important to our Bible story today. Let's pretend to make stew.

- Give each child a bowl and a spoon.

ASK: What should we put in our stew?

- Show the children the plastic food and the unbreakable items you have collected.

- Encourage the children to add the items they think would be good in stew to their bowl. Encourage them to "eat" their stew.

Into the Bible

Time for the Bible Story

SAY: Let's pretend that we are visiting Isaac and Rebekah in our Story Area. We want to see their twin sons now that they have grown up.

- Sing the following song to the tune of "She'll Be Coming 'Round the Mountain" as the children move. End the song in your large group area.

SING: Oh, Isaac and Rebekah had two sons.
Oh, Isaac and Rebekah had two sons.
Oh, the first son was named Esau, and the second was named Jacob.
Oh, Isaac and Rebekah had two sons.

- Have the children sit down.

SAY: Today, our Bible story is about Isaac and Rebekah's twins, Jacob and Esau.

Open the Bible

Supplies: Bible Basics Storybook—pp. 32-33

- Tell the children the story "The Birthright."

Experience the Bible Story

Supplies: CEB Bible; Bible Story Leaflets—Session 11, pp. 2-3

- Show the children the Bible.

TODAY'S BIBLE TOOL: The books of the Bible have many chapters.

SAY: Our Bible story today is from the Old Testament. It is in a book named Genesis. Genesis is divided into many chapters. The first chapter tells the story of Creation.

- Show the children the first chapter of Genesis.

SAY: Today, our story is from chapter 25.

- Show the children Genesis 25.

- Have the children put on the Jacob and Esau puppet they made earlier. Show the children how to hold the puppet so that Jacob faces out. Then have the children turn the puppet so that Esau faces out.

- Place the leaflet inside the Bible. Tell the children the story "The Birthright" from the leaflet, and encourage them to hold up the puppet with Jacob facing out when they hear Jacob's name and with Esau facing out when they hear Esau's name.

ASK: Do you think Esau made a good choice when he sold his birthright?

Say the Bible Verse

Supplies: Class Pack—p. 3, Leader Guide—p. 90

• Show the children the Bible verse picture (Class Pack). Repeat the verse.

• Teach the children signs in American Sign Language to go along with the verse (Leader Guide).

• Encourage the children to make the signs as they say the verse again.

Bible Connections

Explain Birthright

Supplies: none

• Have the children move to an open area of the room.

SAY: Jacob and Esau were twins, but Esau was born first. He was the older son.

• Choose one child to be Esau and another child to be Jacob. Have the children stand side by side in the open area.

• Choose several other children to pretend to be sheep, goats, and camels. Have these children stand behind Esau.

SAY: Because Esau was the older son, he was supposed to grow up to be the leader of the family. He was supposed to get more of the money, land, sheep, goats, and camels. That was Esau's birthright.

• Choose a child to pretend to stir a bowl of stew. Have this child stand behind Jacob.

SAY: Because Jacob was the younger son, he would never be the leader. He would get very little money and land and very few sheep, goats, and camels.

ASK: Who has more sheep, goats, and camels right now?

SAY: In our story today, Esau traded his birthright to Jacob for a bowl of stew.

• Have the child pretending to stir a bowl of stew move behind Esau. Have the children playing the animals move behind Jacob.

ASK: Who has the more sheep, goats, and camels now? Do you think Esau made a good trade?

Bowl-a-rama

Supplies: paper bowl

• Have the children sit in a circle on the floor.

SAY: Let's pretend that the stew Jacob sold to Esau is in this bowl.

• Sing "Isaac and Rebekah Had Two Sons" (lyrics on p. 69). Have the children pass the bowl around the circle as you sing.

• Stop singing. Have the child with the bowl stand up and say the Bible verse after you.

• Continue the game until every child has been "caught" with the bowl.

Live the Bible

Ready, Set...

Supplies: none

• Have the children line up on one side of the room. Make sure the area is clear.

SAY: Esau was not very patient. He was so hungry that he could not wait to eat. Let's see how patient we can be when we play this game. Start running after I say, "Ready, set, go!" The first person to reach the opposite side of the room wins, but you can't start running until I say the word *go*. Ready, set, gosh!

• Keep saying words that sound similar to the word *go* in place of the word itself. Make the children wait before you say, "Ready, set, go!"

ASK: Was it hard to wait?

SAY: Being patient isn't always easy, but it was the key to winning this game. Esau wasn't patient, and he lost his birthright because of his impatience.

Decorate a Stew Bowl

Supplies: paper bowls, glue, small pieces of colored tissue paper, stickers

SAY: Let's make stew bowls to help us remember today's Bible story.

• Give each child a paper bowl.

• Encourage each child to decorate the outside of his or her bowl by gluing on small pieces of colored tissue paper and adding stickers.

Express Praise

Praise and Pray

Supplies: CD-ROM, CD player

• Sing with the children the song "Hear Us As We Pray" from the CD-ROM (lyrics on p. 87). Encourage the children to name any prayer requests.

PRAY: Thank you, God, for always being with us. Amen.

Blessing

Supplies: Leader Guide—p. 12 or earth ball

• Have the children sit in a circle.

• Hand the ball to one child. Have that child stand up.

TIP: If you do not have an earth ball, photocopy "God Created the World" and use the picture in place of the ball.

SAY: *(Child's name)*, you are a blessing to every family of earth.

• Have the child give the ball to the next child in the circle. Have that child stand. Bless that child. Continue until you have blessed each child.

Twins

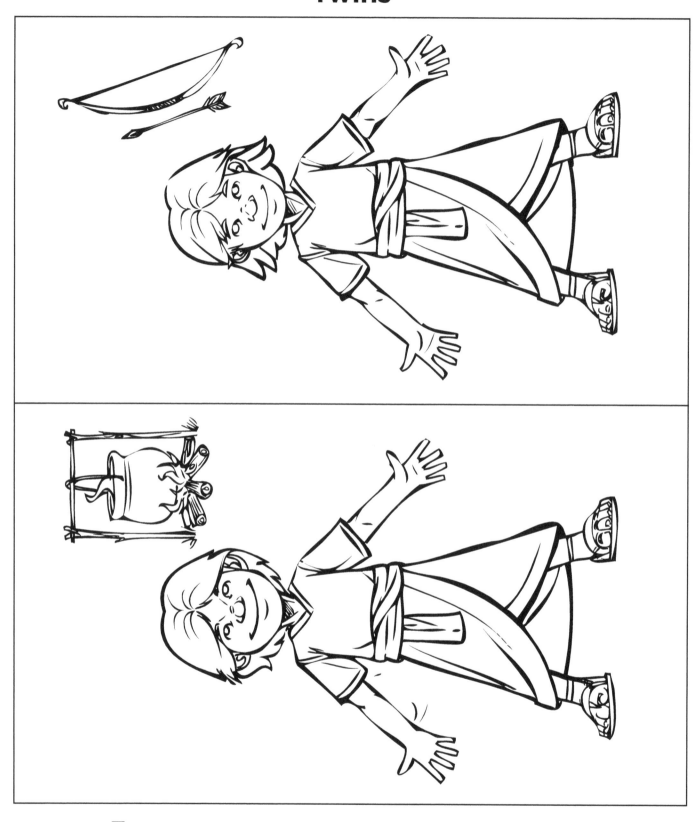

Every family of earth will be blessed because of you
and your descendants. (Genesis 28:14)

Permission is granted to duplicate this page for local church use only. © 2019 Abingdon Press.

The Blessing

Bible Verse: Every family of earth will be blessed because of you and your descendants. (Genesis 28:14)

Bible Story: Genesis 27:1-46

Bible Background

Last week, we heard the story of Esau selling his birthright to Jacob in exchange for a bowl of stew. Genesis 27 tells the story of Rebekah and Jacob conspiring to make Isaac bless Jacob instead of Esau. The story is complex, and none of its participants seem to be clearly right or wrong.

Rebekah, overhearing Isaac's intent to bless Esau, helped Jacob trick Isaac into blessing Jacob instead. On the one hand, Rebekah acted deceitfully to cheat her older son and lie to her husband. But God had told Rebekah when she was pregnant with the twins that one day the older son would serve the younger son. Rebekah may have thought she was acting in order to ensure God's plan was carried out.

Jacob went along with Rebekah's plan, even lying to his father when Isaac asked him directly if he was Esau. Like Rebekah, Jacob acted deceitfully. However, Esau did agree to give Jacob his birthright; therefore, Jacob may have felt justified in tricking his father into blessing him instead.

As for Isaac, it seems incredible that he could really be convinced that Jacob was Esau. Did he allow himself to be duped because he was unhappy with Esau for marrying Canaanite women (Genesis 26:34-35)?

And then there was Esau. His mother and his twin brother worked together to cheat him out of his father's blessing. On the other hand, Esau had sold his birthright to Jacob already. Was he planning to go back on his word?

The story reads like a soap opera! Family relationships are messy. However, as confusing as life is, one thing is certain—God is present.

Devotion

As you prepare to teach today's lesson, take some time to reflect on your blessings. How have you been blessed through the teaching of this class? Read Numbers 6:24-26. Spend time in prayer, thanking God for your blessings. Also, take a moment to pray for God's blessing on each child in your class. Blessings are important and powerful. You may never know how your presence blesses the lives of the children in your class.

biblestorybasics.com

BASIC

Plan

Bible Beginnings
Welcome
Picture the Bible Story
Bible Puzzle
Bible Play

Into the Bible
Time for the Bible Story
Open the Bible
Experience the Bible Story
Say the Bible Verse

Bible Connections
Esau's Arms
Texture Art

Live the Bible
I Spy a Blessing Who…
Experience a Guided
   Blessing

Express Praise
Praise and Pray
Blessing

Bible Beginnings

Welcome

Supplies: Class Pack—Attendance Chart, p. 3; CD-ROM; CD player; tape; offering basket

• Display the attendance chart (Class Pack) and "Unit 3 Bible Verse Picture" (Class Pack—p. 3) at the children's eye level.

• Play "The B-I-B-L-E" from the CD-ROM (lyrics on p. 86) as you welcome each child.

• Have each child mark his or her attendance.

• Show the children where to place their offerings on the worship table.

SAY: Our Bible story today is another story about Jacob and Esau.

• Point out the Bible verse picture, and say the Bible verse for the children.

Picture the Bible Story

Supplies: Leader Guide—p. 78, crayons or markers

• Photocopy "The Blessing" for each child.

• Give each child the picture. Point out the fur wrapped around Jacob's arms.

SAY: This is a picture of Jacob and his father, Isaac. Isaac was almost blind, so Jacob wrapped fur around his arms to trick Isaac into thinking Jacob was Esau.

• Encourage the children to decorate the picture with crayons or markers.

Bible Puzzle

Supplies: Bible Story Leaflets—Session 12, p. 4; crayons or markers

• Give each child a copy of today's Bible Story Leaflet.

SAY: Jacob wanted to trick Isaac into thinking Jacob was Esau. Esau was very hairy, so Jacob wrapped fur around his arms. Isaac thought he was feeling Esau's hairy arms.

• Encourage the children to circle the pictures of things that are furry.

Bible Play

Supplies: bag, unbreakable items that the children can feel

• Place the unbreakable items into the bag.

SAY: Guessing what something is by touch is very important to today's Bible story. Let's try a game where we use only our sense of touch.

• Have a child close his or her eyes and reach a hand into the bag. Let the child feel an item in the bag.

ASK: How does this thing feel? What do you think it is?

• Let the child guess the item, and then have the child remove the item from the bag.

• Give each child a turn. Continue the game with different items.

Into the Bible

Time for the Bible Story

SAY: Let's pretend that we are visiting Isaac and Rebekah in our Story Area. We want to see their twin sons now that they have grown up.

• Sing the following song to the tune of "She'll Be Coming 'Round the Mountain" as the children move. End the song in your large group area.

SING: Oh, Isaac and Rebekah had two sons.
Oh, Isaac and Rebekah had two sons.
Oh, the first son was named Esau, and the second was named Jacob.
Oh, Isaac and Rebekah had two sons.

• Have the children sit down.

SAY: Today, our Bible story is about Isaac and Rebekah's twins, Jacob and Esau.

Open the Bible

Supplies: Bible Basics Storybook—pp. 34-35

• Tell the children the story "The Blessing."

Experience the Bible Story

Supplies: CEB Bible; Bible Story Leaflets—Session 12, pp. 2-3

• Show the children the Bible.

TODAY'S BIBLE TOOL: The books of the Bible have many chapters.

SAY: Our Bible story today is from the Old Testament. It is in a book named Genesis. Genesis is divided into many chapters. The first chapter tells the story of Creation.

• Show the children the first chapter of Genesis.

SAY: Today, our story is from chapter 27.

• Show the children Genesis 27.

SAY: Listen and watch as I tell the story. You can help me do some motions.

• Place the leaflet inside the Bible. Tell the children the story "The Blessing" from the leaflet, and encourage them to do the suggested motions with you.

ASK: Why do you think Jacob tricked his father?

Say the Bible Verse

Supplies: Class Pack—p. 3, Leader Guide—p. 90

• Show the children the Bible verse picture (Class Pack). Repeat the verse.

• Teach the children signs in American Sign Language to go along with the verse (Leader Guide).

• Encourage the children to make the signs as they say the verse again.

Bible Connections

Esau's Arms

Supplies: masking tape, cotton balls

SAY: Jacob tricked his father into giving Jacob the blessing by pretending to be Esau. Let's make our own hairy arms and see if we can guess one another's names.

• Wrap masking tape with the sticky side up around each child's wrists to make cuffs. Spread cotton balls out on a table or rug.

• Let the children press their taped wrists onto the cotton balls to make the balls stick to the tape.

• Have the children sit in a circle. Choose one child to be the guesser. Have the guesser sit in the middle of the circle and close his or her eyes.

• Quietly choose another child from the circle. Have the second child go to the guesser and hold out her or his wrists. Have the second child ask, "Who am I?" Let the guesser touch the second child's wrists.

• Allow the guesser three guesses. Then let the second child become the guesser, and choose another child to hold out his or her wrists to the new guesser.

• Continue until each child has been the guesser.

Texture Art

Supplies: construction paper; glue; items with different textures such as cotton balls, pieces of soft cloth or fake fur, sandpaper, shiny paper, and ribbons

• Give each child a piece of construction paper.

SAY: The texture of something is how it feels to the touch. Texture was very important in today's Bible story. Because Isaac couldn't see, he had to feel Jacob's arms to know whether he was Jacob or Esau.

• Let the children glue items with different textures onto their papers.

Live the Bible

I Spy a Blessing Who...

Supplies: none

• Have the children stand in a circle.

SAY: We're all blessed by God, but we also can be blessings to other people. I'm going to describe someone in our circle who is a blessing. If I'm describing you, remain standing. If I'm not describing you, sit down and try to guess whom I am describing.

• Begin describing a child using sentences that start with "I spy a blessing who..." For example, you might say, "I spy a blessing who is wearing blue. I spy a blessing who is wearing blue and has short hair. I spy a blessing who is wearing blue, has short hair, and has tennis shoes on."

- Continue describing the child until he or she is the only child standing.

SAY: *(Child's name)*, thank you for being a blessing.

- Have the children stand up again, and continue playing the game.

Experience a Guided Blessing

Supplies: none

- Invite the children to sit on the floor, with enough space between them that each child can stretch out his or her arms to either side.

- Read the following meditation slowly.

> Sit on the floor. Close your eyes. Take a deep breath in, and slowly let it out. Continue to breath normally.
>
> Place your hands on the ground in front of you. Think about the things you do in the morning, like waking up and eating breakfast. Thank God for the opportunity to wake up to a new day every morning.
>
> Now stretch your arms out to either side. Open your arms wide, as if you could hold the whole world. Wiggle your fingers back and forth. Think about the things you do during the middle of the day—playing with friends, eating lunch, and going to school or staying home. Thank God for the middle of the day.
>
> Now stretch your arms up above your head. Reach way up! Imagine you can touch the sky. Think about all of the things you do in the evening—eating dinner, being with your family, and going to bed. Thank God for evenings.
>
> Take a deep breath. Keep your eyes closed as we pray. Thank you, God, for the many ways we are blessed throughout every day. Amen.

Express Praise

Praise and Pray

Supplies: CD-ROM, CD player

- Sing with the children the song "Hear Us As We Pray" from the CD-ROM (lyrics on p. 87). Encourage the children to name any prayer requests.

PRAY: Thank you, God, for your many blessings. Amen.

Blessing

Supplies: Leader Guide—p. 12 or earth ball

- Have the children sit in a circle.

- Hand the ball to one child. Have that child stand up.

TIP: If you do not have an earth ball, photocopy "God Created the World" and use the picture in place of the ball.

SAY: *(Child's name)*, you are a blessing to every family of earth.

- Have the child give the ball to the next child in the circle. Have that child stand. Bless that child. Continue until you have blessed each child.

The Blessing

Every family of earth will be blessed because of you
and your descendants. (Genesis 28:14)

Permission is granted to duplicate this page for local church use only. © 2019 Abingdon Press.

Jacob's Dream

Bible Verse: Every family of earth will be blessed because of you and your descendants. (Genesis 28:14)

Bible Story: Genesis 28:10-22

biblestorybasics.com

Bible Background

As we encounter Jacob in today's Bible story, he is on the run. After tricking his father, Isaac, into giving him the blessing meant for his older brother, Esau, Jacob was no longer safe to remain at home. In order to escape Esau's plan to kill him, Jacob left to live with his mother's family.

Today's Bible story is the first story about Jacob without his twin brother. Whether he should have or not, Jacob received the blessing from Isaac. This marks the transition in Genesis from Isaac's story to Jacob's story.

As Jacob headed for Haran, he stopped along the way for the night. While he was asleep, God appeared to Jacob in a dream. God's message to Jacob was a promise. Like God had done for his grandfather Abraham, God promised Jacob land, many descendants, and protection. Jacob also was promised God's presence, now and always.

When Jacob awoke from his dream, he realized its significance. Being on the run as he was, Jacob likely was afraid and uncertain of his future. God's promise always to be with him changed everything. Although Jacob no doubt knew he would encounter challenges, he knew he could count on God to see him through.

When Jacob awoke from his dream encounter with God, he thought, "The LORD is definitely in this place, but I didn't know it" (Genesis 28:16). Growing up as Isaac's son and Abraham's grandson, Jacob certainly had been taught about God. Through this encounter with God, Jacob claimed his own relationship with God.

Devotion

What is your relationship with God? Do you claim God as your own? God wants to claim you. This reassurance is good news to us, who may find ourselves faltering. The promise to Jacob is also a promise to us. God is always with us no matter what happens or where we go. With this lesson, help children—and yourself—understand that, even when we separate ourselves from God, God calls us back and desires to love and bless us.

Bible Beginnings

Welcome

Supplies: Class Pack—Attendance Chart, p. 3; CD-ROM; CD player; tape; offering basket

• Display the attendance chart (Class Pack) and "Unit 3 Bible Verse Picture" (Class Pack—p. 3) at the children's eye level.

• Play "The B-I-B-L-E" from the CD-ROM (lyrics on p. 86) as you welcome each child.

• Have each child mark his or her attendance.

• Show the children where to place their offerings on the worship table.

SAY: Today, our Bible story is about Jacob and an important dream.

• Point out the Bible verse picture, and say the Bible verse for the children.

Picture the Bible Story

Supplies: Leader Guide—p. 84, crayons or markers

• Photocopy "Jacob's Dream" for each child.

• Give each child the picture.

SAY: Jacob dreamed an important dream. While he was dreaming, he heard God speaking to him.

• Encourage the children to decorate the picture with crayons or markers.

Bible Puzzle

Supplies: Bible Story Leaflets—Session 13, p. 4; crayons or markers

• Give each child a copy of today's Bible Story Leaflet.

• Encourage the children to draw a line between each pair of matching angels.

SAY: Jacob dreamed an important dream. Jacob dreamed he saw angels walking up and down a staircase.

Bible Play

Supplies: black construction paper, white crayons, star stickers

• Give each child a piece of black construction paper and a white crayon.

SAY: Today, our Bible story happens at night. Let's draw a nighttime picture.

• Encourage the children to use the white crayon to draw a nighttime scene.

• Let the children add star stickers to their scene.

Into the Bible

Time for the Bible Story

SAY: Let's pretend that we are visiting Jacob in our Story Area.

• Sing the following song to the tune of "She'll Be Coming 'Round the Mountain" as the children move. End the song in your large group area.

SING: Oh, Isaac and Rebekah had two sons.
Oh, Isaac and Rebekah had two sons.
Oh, the first son was named Esau, and the second was named Jacob.
Oh, Isaac and Rebekah had two sons.

• Have the children sit down.

Open the Bible

Supplies: Bible Basics Storybook—pp. 36-37

• Tell the children the story "Jacob's Dream."

Experience the Bible Story

Supplies: CEB Bible; Bible Story Leaflets—Session 13, pp. 2-3

• Show the children the Bible.

TODAY'S BIBLE TOOL: The books of the Bible have many chapters.

SAY: Our Bible story today is from the Old Testament. It is in a book named Genesis. Genesis is divided into many chapters. The first chapter tells the story of Creation.

• Show the children the first chapter of Genesis.

SAY: Today, our story is from chapter 28.

• Show the children Genesis 28.

SAY: Listen and watch as I tell the story. You can help me do some motions.

• Place the leaflet inside the Bible. Tell the children the story "Jacob's Dream" from the leaflet, and encourage them to do the suggested motions with you.

ASK: How do you think Jacob felt when he woke up from the dream?

Say the Bible Verse

Supplies: Class Pack—p. 3, Leader Guide—p. 90

• Show the children the Bible verse picture (Class Pack). Repeat the verse.

• Teach the children signs in American Sign Language to go along with the verse (Leader Guide).

• Encourage the children to make the signs as they say the verse again.

Bible Connections

Hop the Stairs

Supplies: masking tape

• Use masking tape to create "stairs" on the floor in an open area.

SAY: In today's Bible story, Jacob was traveling and stopped for the night to sleep. He slept on the ground with a rock for a pillow. While Jacob slept, he had a dream. In the dream, Jacob saw angels going up and down a tall staircase.

• Have the children line up at the "bottom" of the stairs.

• Encourage the first child in line to hop "up" the stairs and stop at the "top."

• Have the child say the Bible verse, and then have the child hop "down" the stairs.

• Repeat until each child has hopped up and down the stairs.

Say the Story

Supplies: none

• Have the children move to an open area of the room.

• Say the following action poem, and lead the children in doing the motions. You can also sing the poem to the tune of "The Farmer in the Dell."

Oh, Jacob had a dream.
(Press your hands together, and rest your cheek on your hands.)
Oh, Jacob had a dream.
As he slept upon the ground,
(Touch the ground.)
Oh, Jacob had a dream.
(Press your hands together, and rest your cheek on your hands.)

Oh, Jacob had a dream.
(Press your hands together, and rest your cheek on your hands.)
Oh, Jacob had a dream.
He saw a staircase to heaven.
(Stretch your arms up high over your head.)
Oh, Jacob had a dream.
(Press your hands together, and rest your cheek on your hands.)

Oh, Jacob had a dream.
(Press your hands together, and rest your cheek on your hands.)
Oh, Jacob had a dream.
There were angels on the staircase.
(Wave your arms like angel wings.)

Oh, Jacob had a dream.
(Press your hands together, and rest your cheek on your hands.)
Oh, Jacob had a dream.
(Press your hands together, and rest your cheek on your hands.)
Oh, Jacob had a dream.
God spoke to Jacob in the dream.
(Shake your index finger.)
Oh, Jacob had a dream.
(Press your hands together, and rest your cheek on your hands.)

Oh, Jacob had a dream.
(Press your hands together, and rest your cheek on your hands.)
Oh, Jacob had a dream.
God said, "I'll always be with you."
(Point to yourself.)
Oh, Jacob had a dream.
(Press your hands together, and rest your cheek on your hands.)

Live the Bible

Paint a Rock

Supplies: plastic table covering, smocks, rocks, washable paint, paintbrushes

• Cover the table with the covering. Have the children wear smocks.

SAY: Jacob stopped to sleep after traveling all day. He slept on the ground with a rock for a pillow. Let's paint rocks to help us remember today's story.

• Give each child a rock. Let the children paint their rock however they wish.

Rock Pillow

Supplies: Leader Guide—p. 93, crayons or markers, colored tape, cotton balls

• Photocopy "Rock Pillow" twice for each child. Give each child two copies.

SAY: Jacob was using a rock as a pillow when God told him, "I am always with you." Let's make softer pillows to remind us that God is always with us.

• Have each child decorate his or her pictures with crayons or markers.

• Help each child stack the pictures so that the blank sides face each other. Use colored tape to tape three edges of the pictures together, creating a pocket.

• Show the children how to stuff cotton balls inside the pocket, and then help each child tape the fourth edge of the pictures together to complete the pillow.

Express Praise

Praise and Pray

Supplies: CD-ROM, CD player

• Sing with the children the song "Hear Us As We Pray" from the CD-ROM (lyrics on p. 87). Encourage the children to name any prayer requests.

PRAY: Thank you, God, for always being with us. Amen.

Blessing

Supplies: Bible Story Leaflets—Thanksgiving Send-Home, Leader Guide—p. 12 or earth ball

• Have the children sit in a circle.

• Hand the ball to one child. Have that child stand up.

TIP: If you do not have an earth ball, photocopy "God Created the World" and use the picture in place of the ball.

SAY: *(Child's name)*, you are a blessing to every family of earth.

• Have the child give the ball to the next child in the circle. Have that child stand. Bless that child. Continue until you have blessed each child.

• Mail "Happy Thanksgiving!" to each child this week.

Jacob's Dream

Every family of earth will be blessed because of you
and your descendants. (Genesis 28:14)

Permission is granted to duplicate this page for local church use only. © 2019 Abingdon Press.

Ministry with Kids with Special Needs

by Brittany Sky

According to the U.S. Census Bureau, there are approximately 57 million people in the United States with disabilities. That means about one in five Americans has a disability of some sort. With this kind of number of children being diagnosed with some kind of learning disability or special need, we as a church must accept that children in our classrooms will be part of that sociological makeup. We are called to "let the children come." All children are included in this invitation. We must learn how to meet the needs of these children and their families. One of the easiest and most effective things you can do as a teacher is adjust the way you manage your classroom. Here are some helpful classroom management tips that will help all the students in your room.

1. Be in contact with the guardians of the children in your classroom. They will know their child better than anyone else. They will be able to tell you what works best for their child at home, at school, and in social activities. They can give you suggestions on how to work with their child.

2. Post the rules and expectations where the class can see them. Make sure the rules are written in "We will" statements and not "We will not" statements. If you provide only what your class will not do, the children will not know what the class will do. With each written rule, provide a picture of what that behavior or action looks like.

3. Provide a visual schedule of the class session. What will your class be doing that day? Giving this information to your children will help them stay focused and attentive.

4. Have a box of "fidget toys" available for your class. It can help your children to have something to touch and manipulate while they listen. Some suggested fidget toys include play dough, chenille stems, Slinkys®, stress balls, Klixx®, or Magic Loops®.

5. Use a timer in your classroom with each activity. The timer will help everyone in the room stay focused because they will know that they have to focus only for the amount of time you give them.

6. Provide a small tent or a quiet space in the classroom. This will provide the children a space to go if they feel overloaded and are in need of some quiet time. Place books, crayons and paper, and prayer stones in this space.

7. If you know you have a child who has a hard time focusing, invite that child to sit in a place where he or she will be sure to see you. This will help the child maintain focus and feel more included.

8. Provide movement breaks during class. Turn on music and dance out the wiggles, stretch, or go for a quick walk around your classroom.

Permission is granted to duplicate this page for local church use only. © 2019 Abingdon Press.

The B-I-B-L-E

Theme Song

The B-I-B-L-E
Yes, that's the book for me.
I stand alone on the Word of God.
The B-I-B-L-E

B-I-B-L-E (4x)

It starts in Genesis with the Creation
And ends when Jesus returns in Revelation.
And in between the greatest story ever told,
Of Jesus' love for you and me that never lets
    us go.

Open up the Word, and you'll see
God's plan for you and me.

The B-I-B-L-E, B-I-B-L-E
I stand alone on the Word of God.
The B-I-B-L-E
The B-I-B-L-E, B-I-B-L-E
I stand alone on the Word of God.
The B-I-B-L-E

For every tongue and tribe, for every nation,
It's the gospel of the one who brings salvation.
And one day every knee will bow before the
    throne.
Until then we've been given everything we
    need to know.

Open up the Word, and you'll see
God's plan for you and me.

The B-I-B-L-E, B-I-B-L-E
I stand alone on the Word of God.
The B-I-B-L-E
The B-I-B-L-E, B-I-B-L-E
I stand alone on the Word of God.
The B-I-B-L-E

Let's get back to the basics, back to the word,
Back to the greatest news the world's ever
    heard.
Back to the basics, back to the word,
Back to the greatest news the world's ever
    heard.

B-I-B-I-B-L-E

The B-I-B-L E, B-I-B-L-E
I stand alone on the Word of God.
The B-I-B-L-E
The B-I-B-L-E, B-I-B-L-E
I stand alone on the Word of God.
The B-I-B-L-E

Words: Andrew Wilson

Music: Andrew Wilson

© 2019 Andrew Wilson. Used by permission. All rights reserved.

Permission is granted to duplicate this page for local church use only. © 2019 Abingdon Press.

BIBLE STORY BASICS

Hear Us As We Pray

Prayer Song

Lord, we call to you right now.

Hear us as we pray.

Folded hands and quiet hearts

Hear us as we pray.

Give us heroes' hearts.

Reveal your truth today.

Give us strength to do what's good.

Hear us as we pray.

Hear us as we pray.

Lord, we ask this in your name.

Hear us as we pray.

Boldly share, your truth proclaim.

Hear us as we pray.

Give us heroes' hearts

To live your truth each day.

Give us courage in our faith.

Hear us as we pray.

Hear us as we pray.

Lord, we call to you right now.

Hear us as we pray.

Guide our feet and light our way.

Hear us as we pray.

Give us heroes' hearts

In all we do and say.

Give us hope as we seek peace.

Hear us as we pray.

Hear us as we pray.

Hear us as we pray.

Words: Matt Huesmann

Music: Matt Huesmann

© 2017 Matt Huesmann Music. Used by permission. All rights reserved.

Permission is granted to duplicate this page for local church use only. © 2019 Abingdon Press.

Genesis 1:31

Unit 1 Bible Verse Signs

God saw everything he had **made**: it was supremely **good**.

God

Point the index finger of your right hand, with the other fingers curled down. Bring the hand down as if drawing a shepherd's crook while opening the palm.

Saw

Hold your index and middle fingers in a V shape. Touch the V beneath one eye. Move the hand forward.

Everything

Hold your left palm toward your body and your right palm away from your body. Circle the right hand out and around the left palm. End with the back of the right hand in the open palm of the left hand.

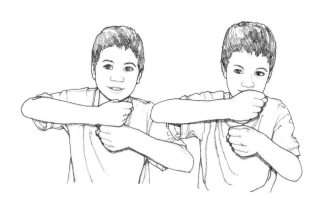

Made

Make fists with both hands. Place the right fist on the left fist. Twist the fists from side to side in opposite directions.

Good

Hold your left palm toward the body. Touch the fingers of your right hand to your chin. Move the right hand forward, and drop it into the open palm of the left hand.

Permission is granted to duplicate this page for local church use only. © 2019 Abingdon Press.

Genesis 15:5

Unit 2 Bible Verse Signs

Look up at the **sky** and count the **stars**... this how many **children** you will have.

Look

Hold your index and middle fingers in a V shape. Touch the V beneath one eye. Move the hand forward.

Sky

Place your right hand out flat in front of your body with your palm facing down. Move your hand over your head in an arc. Follow your hand with your eyes as you move it. Stop the arc in front of your right shoulder.

Stars

Point the index fingers of both hands. Move the hands up and down in front of your face while looking up.

Children

Pretend to pat the heads of two small children.

Permission is granted to duplicate this page for local church use only. © 2019 Abingdon Press.

Genesis 28:14

Unit 3 Bible Verse Signs

Every family of **earth** will be **blessed** because of **you** and your descendants.

Every

Make fists with both hands, and stick your thumbs up from the fists. Hold your hands in front of your body. Brush your right knuckles down your left thumb.

Family

On each hand, touch your index finger to your thumb. Touch the two hands together at the tips of the index fingers, and then circle the hands around so that the little fingers of both hands touch.

Earth

Place your right thumb and right middle finger on the back of your left hand, and rock the right hand back and forth.

Blessed

Make fists with both hands, and hold your thumbs flat on the fists. Touch your hands to your mouth. Move both hands down while opening your fists with your palms facing down.

You

Point an index finger away from yourself.

Permission is granted to duplicate this page for local church use only. © 2019 Abingdon Press.

The Special Tree

Session 3—p. 22

Permission is granted to duplicate this page for local church use only. © 2019 Abingdon Press.

Abraham and Sarah's Tent

Session 7—p. 44

Permission is granted to duplicate this page for local church use only. © 2019 Abingdon Press.

Rock Pillow

Session 13—p. 83

Permission is granted to duplicate this page for local church use only. © 2019 Abingdon Press.

B is for Bible

Use this extra coloring sheet when necessary.

Permission is granted to duplicate this page for local church use only. © 2019 Abingdon Press.

Happy Birthday to You!

Give this coloring sheet to any child celebrating a birthday.

Permission is granted to duplicate this page for local church use only. © 2019 Abingdon Press.

Comments from Users

Let us know what you think! Your comments will help us write a better curriculum for you and the children you teach. Please send your comments and suggestions to:

Daphna Flegal, Children's Unit
The United Methodist Publishing House
2222 Rosa L. Parks Blvd.
Nashville, TN   37228-1306

Please check the components that you use:

_____ Leader Guide _____ Student
_____ Bible Story   Take-Home
                      Leaflets   CD
_____ Class Pack   _____ *Bible Basics*
                                                             Storybook

Use the following scale to rate each of the resources:
N/A = Not Applicable
1 = Never   3 = Most of the Time
2 = Sometimes   4 = All of the Time

Leader Guide

_____ The Leader Guide was easy to use.
_____ Children grew to understand the Bible stories from the suggested activities.
Comments about Leader Guide:

_____
_____
_____

Bible Story Leaflets

_____ The children enjoyed moving to the Bible stories as they were read to them.
Comments about Bible Story Leaflets:

_____
_____
_____

Class Pack

_____ The Bible verse pictures were colorful and engaging for the children.
_____ We used the attendance chart.

Student Take-Home CD

_____ The children enjoyed learning and singing the songs on the CD.

Bible Basics Storybook

_____ The children enjoyed hearing the retellings of the Bible stories.

My favorite activity this quarter was _____
_____

My least favorite activity this quarter was _____
_____

Overall, I would rate this **Fall 2019** quarter: _____
3 = The best that it could possibly be.
2 = Provided some good moments for the children's faith development.
1 = Ineffective with the faith development of the children in my church.

Leader's Name: _____
Church: _____
Address: _____
_____
_____
Phone No.: _____

Permission is granted to duplicate this page for local church use only. © 2019 Abingdon Press.

A perfect gift for the children in your congregation!

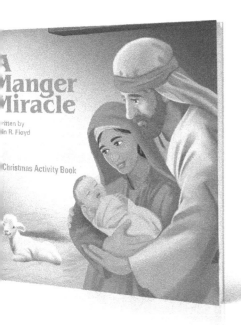

This beautiful Christmas book tells the story of Jesus' birth found in the Gospels of Matthew and Luke. Its colorful illustrations and simple words are perfect for ages 4–7. Includes puzzles, stickers, and a letter to parents. Makes a wonderful gift that children will love!

$199 each

Sold in convenient, affordable packages of 10.

9781501890901

00-672-1789 | Cokesbury.com
all a Resource Consultant

Cokesbury

Bible STORY BASICS

Fall 2019
Vol. 1 • No. 1

EDITORIAL / DESIGN TEAM

Daphna Flegal . . . . Writer/Editor
Lucas Hilliard. . . . . Production Editor
Tim Carlton . . . . .Designer

ADMINISTRATIVE TEAM

Rev. Brian K. Milford. . . . . President and Publisher
Marjorie M. Pon . . . . Associate Publisher and Editor of Church School Publications (CSP)
Mary M. Mitchell . . . . Design Manager
Brittany Sky . . . . Senior Editor, Children's Resources

BIBLE STORY BASICS: PRE-READER, LEADER GUIDE: An official resource for The United Methodist Church approved by Discipleship Ministries and published quarterly by Abingdon Press, a division of The United Methodist Publishing House, 2222 Rosa L. Parks Blvd., Nashville, TN 37228-1306. Price: $14.99. Copyright © 2019 Abingdon Press. All rights reserved. Send address changes to BIBLE STORY BASICS: PRE-READER, LEADER GUIDE, Subscription Services, 2222 Rosa L. Parks Blvd., Nashville, TN 37228-1306 or call 800-672-1789. Printed in the United States of America.

To order copies of this publication, call toll free: **800-672-1789**. You may fax your order to 800-445-8189. Telecommunication Device for the Deaf/Telex Telephone: 800-227-4091. Or order online at *cokesbury.com*. Use your Cokesbury account, American Express, Visa, Discover, or Mastercard.

For information concerning permission to reproduce any material in this publication, write to Rights and Permissions, The United Methodist Publishing House, 2222 Rosa L. Parks Blvd., Nashville, TN 37228-1306. You may fax your request to 615-749-6128. Or email *permissions@umpublishing.org*.

Scripture quotations are taken from the Common English Bible, copyright 2011. Used by permission. All rights reserved.

PACP10557321-01

Abingdon Press™

CPSIA information can be obtained
at www.ICGtesting.com
Printed in the USA
LVHW011117061219
639670LV00002B/2/P